BENEDEIT

The Anglo-Norman voyage of St Brendan

BENEDEIT

The Anglo-Norman
voyage of St Brendan

edited by

IAN SHORT
Westfield College
University of London

and

BRIAN MERRILEES
Victoria College
University of Toronto

MANCHESTER
UNIVERSITY PRESS

© Manchester University Press 1979

All rights reserved

First published 1979
by Manchester University Press
Oxford Road
Manchester M13 9PL

British Library Cataloguing in Publication Data

Benedeit
  The Anglo-Norman 'Voyage of St Brendan'.
  I. Title
  II. Short, Ian *b.1939*
  III. Merrilees, Brian S
  IV. Voyage of St Brendan
  841'.1   PR1834.B/

ISBN 0–7190–0735–6

Phototypeset in V.I.P. Times by
Western Printing Services Ltd, Bristol

Printed in Great Britain
by The Pitman Press, Bath.

Contents

Preface

The purpose of this new edition of the Anglo-Norman *Brendan* is to bring before a wider, and particularly undergraduate public, a poem which, for all its inherent interest and much acclaimed literary merit, has hitherto been available to only a small body of specialists. Professor E. G. R. Waters's classic edition of 1928 has for many years now been out of print and virtually inaccessible to English-speaking readers except in libraries or in expensive reprints. A work of meticulous and exhaustive scholarship, it is unlikely ever to be entirely superseded, and it is certainly not our aim to attempt to do so here. Indeed, the debt which we owe to Waters's edition is, as we freely and gratefully acknowledge, considerable. However, excellent though Waters's *Voyage of St Brendan* is, the methods which he used to establish his text were clearly those of a scholar intent on recreating a literary archetype, and the text which he produced is inevitably more synthetic than real. On closer inspection, for instance, its remarkable metrical regularity proves to have been achieved at the cost of almost six hundred editorial emendations made to the base manuscript. Without wishing to produce a text after the strictly non-interventionist fashion of the Bédierist school, we hope that a newly edited text of the *Brendan* will gain additional utility and justification if it is allowed to reflect more faithfully a medieval literary reality with many—though certainly not all—of its blemishes and idiosyncrasies. There will be those who point out that on methodological grounds the reality of ultimate importance must remain the poem as first written down by Benedeit himself rather than as copied by one of a series of later scribes. While not in the least denying the validity of this view, we would draw attention to two practical considerations in particular: firstly, that there does exist a copy eminently suitable for a single-manuscript edition, and secondly, that for us to have attempted a reconstruction of Benedeit's original would have entailed duplicating in large measure the composite text already printed by Waters. We have, at the same time as producing a new conservative text, endeavoured to keep in mind the needs of the modern reader approaching medieval French perhaps for the first time in the original, and we hope that our introduction, annotations and glossary will contribute to making such an initiation a pleasurable and rewarding experience.

We should like, finally, to record our gratitude to Professor T. B. W. Reid for his thorough and searching criticism of our work. His long experience as a textual scholar has enabled us to improve our edition substantially. For the shortcomings and errors which subsist, we alone are, of course, responsible.

I. S.
B. M.
May 1978

Introduction

THE LEGEND OF ST BRENDAN

The legend of Brendan the Navigator is a Christianised variation on one of the oldest known literary themes, that of the odyssey, a tradition of which the ultimate origins can be traced back, through a common fund of Indo-European folklore and mythology, by way of the Persian *Thousand and One Nights*, the Irish *immrama*, the Latin, Greek and Sumerian epics, to at least the third millennium B.C. and no doubt beyond. It tells of the fabulous adventures that befall St Brendan and his companions during their seven-year sea journey in search of the Promised Land, and is one of the most widely known voyage-tales of the Middle Ages.

Our knowledge of the historical Brendan is scant, and there is no reference to him before the seventh-century *Life of St Columba* by Adomnán. He was evidently born in Kerry in south-west Ireland during the last quarter of the fifth century; he entered the priesthood and followed his calling in Ireland, most notably at Clonfert (Galway). Even though his visit to Wales, and his founding there of the abbey of Llancarfan, probably have as little basis in history as the journeys which he is alleged to have made to Brittany and the Orkney and Shetland Islands, Brendan does seem to have undertaken a voyage to Iona sometime after 563 when he was already an old man, and during his lifetime he may well have acquired a considerable reputation as a traveller. He was also an influential churchman, and a number of religious houses recognised the Abbot of Clonfert as their founder. Several Irish toponyms and at least one in Brittany recall his name. He died in around 577 and was buried in his native Ireland. As in the case of all early Irish saints, the circumstances surrounding his sanctification are obscure.[1]

More detailed and decidedly more colourful is Brendan's legendary biography. In the centuries following his death, his fame as a voyager

seems to have grown as various legendary elements, mostly relating to
seafaring exploits and adventures, came to be associated with his
name. While some of these undoubtedly have their roots in Irish
folklore and literature, others reveal a wider heritage, from the monastic ideals of the early Irish church to Continental traditions of Classical
and biblical literatures. Affinities with the story of Sinbad the Sailor
may even (though not necessarily) point to more exotic influences.
While it is true, therefore, that the surviving corpus of *Brendan* legend
remains unmistakably Celtic, and in particular Irish, in its ethos, it can
also be said to occupy a place within the mainstream of European
literature. Whether such literary cosmopolitanism (which includes the
fact that the earliest surviving texts are in Latin and not the vernacular)
is to be explained by the considerable Irish missionary activity during
the centuries which saw the elaboration of these legends, must remain
an open question.

It is not, however, until the ninth century that the *Brendan* legends
are set down and preserved, though earlier forms of them must certainly have existed. There are two principal texts, each extant in
several versions, which recount Brendan's life and travels: the *Vita
sancti Brendani*, a Latin prose life first composed in the ninth century
in Ireland, and the *Navigatio sancti Brendani*, also in prose and the
source of the Anglo-Norman poem printed in this edition.[2] There is
some uncertainty over the date and origin of the *Navigatio*, but it
would appear to have been in existence by the beginning of the tenth
century, and to have been the work of an Irish writer. Whether,
however, the author was living in Ireland when he wrote, or, as Carl
Selmer has suggested, in the Frankish province of Lotharingia
(approximately present-day Lorraine and Belgium) is not clear.[3] The
Vita survives in several versions, all but one of them conflated with the
Navigatio story. It tells, amongst other things, of two voyages undertaken by Brendan, the first an unsuccessful attempt over five years to
find a distant island promised him in a vision, the second lasting a
further two years in which his mission is accomplished. It comprises
also ample details of Brendan's ancestry, birth and childhood, his
adoption by St Íde and his education at the hands of Bishop Erc, and is
completed by an account of his life following his return from the
voyages.

The *Navigatio*, on the other hand, is essentially the story of a single,
seven-year voyage (by way of several fantastic islands) with only the
briefest reference to other periods of Brendan's life. The structure of

the *Navigatio* is quite different from that of the *Vita*, which follows more or less faithfully the traditional biographical pattern of saints' lives. The *Navigatio*'s form is that of the Irish *immram* (literally 'rowing about') or voyage-tale, a genre in which a sea journey supplies the framework for recounting a succession of isolated adventures. Three principal Irish *immrama* have survived; all consist of tales of ocean voyages and the visiting of islands, the descriptions of which usually owe more to imagination than to observation.[4] Such legendary voyages are thought to have originated in actual journeys made by Irish seafarers and by Irish monks seeking desert places where they might lead an ascetic and contemplative life,[5] but whatever real substance such accounts may once have contained was soon embroidered with marvellous and fantastic detail in the passage from history to poetic legend. Both in outline and in detail, the Latin *Navigatio* is clearly modelled on the Irish genre, though not specifically on any of the surviving *immrama*. While some scholars have held that one of these vernacular texts, the *Voyage of Mael Duin*, is a source for the *Navigatio* (the two share many striking parallels), it appears more likely that the *Brendan* text provided the basis for the Irish work and that its Christian elements were appropriately secularised.[6] Irish versions of the *Brendan* legends are not lacking, but they are late in date in comparison to the principal Latin texts.[7]

The *Navigatio* was immensely popular during the Middle Ages. Not only do more than 120 Latin manuscripts of the work survive from all over Europe, but there are also several translations and adaptations of it into the medieval vernaculars, of which the Anglo-Norman version is probably the best-known.[8] Benedeit's *Voyage of Brendan* has been recast and adapted into verse, and while some of the episodes and details of the *Navigatio* have been discarded, others have been artistically rearranged in order clearly to enhance the dramatic impact of the narrative.[9] There are three other versions of the *Brendan* in medieval French, one in verse from the thirteenth century, and two prose redactions which appear as chapters in legendaries from the thirteenth to the fifteenth centuries. There is in addition a version in Old Provençal.[10] Of all the French versions, however, Benedeit's Anglo-Norman poem was evidently the most successful, enough indeed for it to have been translated back into Latin in at least one verse and two prose redactions.[11] The popularity of the *Brendan* legend hardly diminished until the voyages of discovery in the fifteenth and sixteenth centuries changed current European concepts of geography.

It hardly needs to be emphasised that the *Navigatio* is much more than a simple voyage-tale. Within its flexible *immram* framework, its narrative successfully synthesises a host of disparate traditions: from Irish myths of a 'happy other world' in the western ocean to Christian visions of heaven and hell, from picturesque details of a hermit being fed by a tame otter to a moving description of Judas's private hell, from an Easter feast on the back of a whale to the bird-incarnations of the same neutral angels that will later reappear in Dante's *Inferno*. Recent scholarship has investigated suggestions of lost apocryphal material too.[12] In the past century and a half, the *Brendan* legend and its transmission have engrossed both professional and amateur students of literature, hagiography, history and—not least—geography. Alongside the many studies of the relationship of the Latin and vernacular texts and of the various aspects of their composition, there exist several analyses of the 'geographical' content of the legend, the more conservative of which seek simply to identify some of the islands visited by the abbot and his monks, while the most ambitious claim to discover in Brendan's imaginative literary journey evidence that Irish sea-wanderers had, before the Vikings, actually reached the North American continent.[13]

BENEDEIT'S VERSION

For evidence as to the date of composition of the Anglo-Norman *Brendan* we need look no further than the first line of the text. This names the poet's patron as Queen Aaliz, who can safely be identified with Adeliza of Louvain who became the second wife of Henry I of England in 1121. However, one manuscript of the four that preserve the prologue of the poem[14] has a variant reading which for Adeliza substitutes *Mahalt*, that is Maud or Matilda, the name this time of King Henry's first wife whom he married in 1100 and who had died in 1118. On whether *Mahalt* or *Aaliz* is to be considered as the authentic reading, and on which queen one assumes to have been the original dedicatee, depends the date to be assigned to the poem. The claims of both queens are good and, as Waters admitted, the choice between them is difficult: both women of course spoke French, though for Adeliza this was her native tongue, while Matilda, who had been born in Scotland, was educated in English convents; both were patronesses of the arts, of poetry in particular.[15] A further clue might be provided by l. 4 of the prologue which speaks of the queen as seeking and encouraging peace in Henry's kingdom, though this may be nothing more than conventional eulogy. Yet it is at least partly on the basis of this consideration that Waters finally opts in favour of Adeliza, arguing that such talk of peace could hardly apply to the first nineteen years of Henry's reign. Professor R. L. G. Ritchie, championing Matilda, countered by maintaining that political expectations in the period immediately following Henry's defeat of his brother in 1106 and his conquest of Normandy could well correspond to those expressed in the prologue.[16] However this may be, and however strong the claims that can be urged for Matilda, there is no clear case for us to reject the reading *Aaliz* from the manuscript that we have selected to edit here. In any case, a dating to the first quarter of the twelfth century—be it *c.* 1106 or *c.* 1121—should be precise enough for most practical purposes.

The choice of patroness and date of composition will naturally be determining factors in any attempt to identify the author who in l. 8 names himself as *li apostoiles danz Benedeiz*. The title *danz* (< Latin DOMINUS) is a feudal term that was relatively widely used in the twelfth century as a form of address for both secular and clerical individuals. It is almost certainly the latter in Benedeit's case, given the source, tone, style and content of his text, and it is quite possible that the title refers in fact to a Benedictine monk. The real crux of this particular line, however, lies in the use of *apostoiles*, the normal meaning of which in Old French is 'pope' but which is clearly not applicable here. Waters suggested that *apostoiles* could be adjectival, meaning 'belonging to a monastery' and reinforcing *danz*. E. Walberg proposed instead to interpret the word as a sobriquet attached to a monk by the name of Benedict, in much the same way as family names such as Leconte were first used without necessarily implying the rank indicated.[17] Walberg's argument, however, depends on inverting the order of the words to read *danz Benedeiz li Apostoiles*. No commentator on the line seems to have been aware of the use of *apostoiles* to designate a papal emissary or envoy which is attested in the Anglo-Norman *Vie de Thomas Becket* by Beneit, and it may be that Benedeit's title refers simply to this particular ecclesiastical function.[18]

No historical person, however, by the name of Benedict or Benedictus can be confidently identified with the author of the Anglo-Norman *Brendan*. Waters mentions, only to dismiss them, two possibilities: a Benedictus who was at one stage chaplain to the Conqueror and later archdeacon of Rouen, and Benedict of Gloucester, author of a Latin life of St Dubricius. Professor Legge has more recently suggested that Benedeit could have been a monk from the Norman abbey of Bec who came to England with Gilbert Crispin, Abbot of Westminster, himself a former resident of Bec. The name of Benedictus evidently figures in Bec records immediately following Gilbert's, and Miss Legge conjectures that he could have been introduced with Gilbert to the court of Queen Matilda by Anselm, Archbishop of Canterbury, a life-long friend of Gilbert's.[19] However the time lapse between Gilbert's departure from Bec about 1085 and the earliest proposed date for the *Brendan*'s composition, 1106, does not increase the plausibility of this Benedict of Bec being the Benedeit of our text. Furthermore, the speculation is based on an acceptance of Ritchie's supposition that Matilda was indeed the patroness of the Anglo-Norman poem. Tempting as it is, therefore, to wish to attribute to our text not only a specific patron but also an exact date of composition, and to provide its author with a particular extra-literary identity, we are forced to conclude that, as with so much medieval vernacular writing, such precision will probably always remain elusive. Suffice it to say that Benedeit's *Brendan* is one of the earliest datable French poems of the twelfth century, and that its immediate insular origin can be assured beyond any reasonable doubt.

MANUSCRIPTS

Six manuscripts of Benedeit's *Brendan* have survived, of which two (*C* and *F*) are fragments:

    A. London, British Library, Cotton Vespasian B. X (I), ff. 1–11. The text is written in double columns of forty-four lines each, 1834 lines in all. The handwriting is a neat and regular cursive with large, alternating blue and red initials, decorated with long vertical tendrils, dividing the poem into thirty-six sections. The first letters of each line are capitals set off marginally from the body of the text. The scribe uses current contractions and introduces acute accents over some vowels and the letter *c*. The only evidence for dating the volume is palaeographic, and the majority of scholars have attributed it to the thirteenth century (some even to the twelfth). However N. R. Ker (*Medieval Libraries of Great Britain*, 2nd ed., London, 1964, p. 73) considers it to belong to the first half of the fourteenth century, which would be quite in accord both with the decorative style of its initials and the hooked ascenders on certain of its letter forms. It was at one stage, as Ker has also shown, in the library of the cathedral priory of Durham. It also contains, on ff. 11v–21, a text of the Latin *Navigatio sancti Brendani*. A diplomatic transcription of the Anglo-Norman poem was published by H. Suchier in *Romanische Studien* [Strasbourg] 5 (1875), 553–88. This Ms. formed the base of Francisque Michel's (1878) and Waters's (1928) editions, as it does of ours.

B. Paris, Bibliothèque Nationale, nouv. acq. fr. 4503, ff. 19v–42. Contains also *inter alia* the Old French *Alexis* (Ms. *A* of C. Storey's 1968 edition), and Clemence of Barking's *Vie de sainte Catherine* (Ms. *A* of W. MacBain's 1964 edition). Dates from the end of the twelfth or beginning of the thirteenth century; lacks 169 lines (two others added); Anglo-Norman origin.

C. Oxford, Bodleian, Rawl. D 913, f. 85. Fragment consisting of a single folio corresponding to ll. 1–310 of our edition (with one couplet missing). Late twelfth or early thirteenth century; Anglo-Norman.

D. York, Minster Library, xvi. K. 12 (I), ff. 23–36. Contains also the text of Marie de France's *Fables* (Ms. *Y* of A. Ewert and R. C. Johnston's 1966 edition). Twelve lines are missing and nine not found elsewhere are added. Late twelfth or early thirteenth century; Anglo-Norman.

E. Paris, Bibliothèque de l'Arsenal, 3516, ff. 96–100v. Modernising revision in Continental French of the second half of the thirteenth century (1267–8); some Picard dialect forms; 1757 lines only; diplomatic edition by Th. Auracher in *Zeitschrift für romanische Philologie* 2 (1878), 438–57.

F. Cologny-Genève, Fondation Martin Bodmer, 17. This is a fragment of four single-column leaves preserving lines corresponding to ll. 792–889, 1165–81, and 1184–202 of our edition. It seems to be the oldest Ms. of our poem extant, dating in all probability from the last part of the twelfth century. The hand is insular and somewhat crude. The fragment is illustrated, described and the text transcribed by F. Vielliard, *Bibliotheca Bodmeriana: Manuscrits français du Moyen Age*, (Cologny-Genève, 1975), pp. 167–70. This Ms. is the only one of the six that was unknown to Waters.

The relationship between the first five of these Mss. was discussed in some detail by Waters (ch. iv) who classifed them into a stemma, which it would not be appropriate to discuss here. Suffice it to say that he found links on the one hand between *A* and *B*, and on the other between *D* and *E*, with *C* deriving, in his view, independently from the original. As for fragment *F*, a comparison of common readings provides insufficient evidence for classifying it exclusively either with the *AB* or with the *DE* group (it does not overlap with the *C* fragment). It contains a number of independent variants. For our present purposes, it is enough to note, with Waters (p. x), that *A* 'is the completest and best Ms.', and that its preservation of many of the archaisms of the original as well as its general artistic coherence make it the obvious choice for a single-manuscript edition such as ours.

VERSIFICATION

Benedeit's is, in all probability, the earliest surviving French poem to be written in what was later to become the standard verse form of courtly romance, the octosyllabic rhyming couplet (eight-syllable lines rhyming in pairs). There is, however, one essential difference between the Continental octosyllable and what we may term its insular prototype:[20] whereas any final unstressed *e* of a line became supernumerary in the former, in Benedeit's prosody it retained full syllabic value:

> 1 2 3 4 5 6 7 8
> Par qui creistrat lei de terre
> 1 2 3 4 5 6 7 8
> E remandrat tante guerre. [3–4]

In the *Brendan* the octosyllable has a particular regularity. The large majority of lines have an identifiable internal structure which divides each octosyllable into two equal portions or hemistichs, mostly by the coincidence of an accented fourth syllable and the end of a word (e.g. 1, 2, 3 *et passim*), occasionally by an unstressed fourth syllable also ending a word (the so-called lyric caesura: e.g. 5, 8, 20). This medial break appears, however, not to be so rigorously applied as to constitute an obligatory caesura (e.g. 112, 576). The verse line is further reinforced by its use as the basic syntactic unit of the text, and only very occasionally does the sentence structure overflow from one line into the next, e.g. 177–8, 335–7, 1519–20.

Anglo-Norman texts later than the *Brendan* are often marked by an imperfect syllable-count in a large number of otherwise unexceptionable lines of verse, a characteristic shared by our Ms. *A* which has many lines with more or fewer than the expected eight syllables. Often, of course, spelling can obscure what is in reality a correct octosyllable: words ending in an unstressed *e*, for example, consistently lose it by elision if followed elsewhere than at the medial break by a word beginning with a vowel:

> N(e) entr(e) eols nen unt amur ne fai. [70]

Among the more common words which normally elide their vowels in this way are *ne*, *de*, *se*, *que*, and the singular definite articles *le* and *li*, e.g. *d(e) or e d(e) argent* 291, *l(e) ordre* 34, *l(i) abes* 39 etc. But in nearly all such cases there is considerable fluctuation in Benedeit's usage, and here at least elision is probably to be regarded simply as a poetic licence available to the poet if and when he needed it. Elision seems to be regularly prevented, however, by the retention of the dental in the unstressed verbal termination *-et*, e.g.

> $\overset{1}{\text{C}}\overset{2}{\text{u}}\text{m}\overset{3}{\text{a}}\text{nd}\overset{4}{\text{e}}\text{t}\overset{5}{\text{e}}\text{a}\overset{6}{\text{l}}\overset{78}{\text{s lui obeïr.}}$ [151]

In addition, while some verb forms in our text drop their internal unstressed *e*, e.g. *frat* 367, *fras* 426, *truvrat* 1766, others retain a graphical *e* with no syllabic value, particularly between *v* and *r*, e.g.

> Quant av(e)rez vent, siglez sulunc [227]
> Viv(e)re trovet e vestement. [956]

Other vowels traditionally in hiatus undergo contraction in our text, e.g.

> $\overset{1}{\text{P}}\overset{2}{\text{o}}\text{ür (o)}\overset{3}{\text{u}}\text{ss}\overset{4}{\text{e}}\text{nt n}\overset{5}{\text{e}}\text{ f}\overset{6}{\text{u}}\text{st }\overset{7}{\text{l'a}}\overset{8}{\text{b}}\text{it.}$ [655]

Enclitic forms are occasionally written out in full, as for example *en le vis* 1453 where the two words count for one syllable (cf. *el nun* 131). *Espirit* and *angele*, despite their spelling, are treated as two-syllable words.[21]

But even when allowance is made for such orthographic peculiarities, and for the existence of words which conventionally have two interchangeable forms (e.g. *cum/cume*, *or/ore*, *cil/icil* etc.), there remain a significant proportion of lines in Ms. *A* whose syllabic count is irregular. The fact that the vast majority of these could, if necessary, be 'corrected' with minimal editorial intervention would seem to indicate that they are to be imputed to succesive scribes rather than to the original poet, though it should be noted that none of the other extant Mss. presents a completely regular set of octosyllabic lines.

As for the rhymes, apart from a few phonetic peculiarities (see p. 12 below), their most noteworthy feature is the relatively high frequency of leonine rhymes, that is rhymes in which not only the consonant preceding the tonic vowel is identical (rich rhymes), but also the vowel preceding that consonant (-vcv̌), e.g. *vetheir* : *setheir* 55, *enveiat* : *aveiat* 139, *sujurnerent* : *turnerent* 325. Waters has calculated that over twenty-seven per cent of all Benedeit's rhymes are rich, and that most of these (twenty per cent of the total number of rhymes) are leonine.[22]

Benedeit is generally regarded as a careful and skilful versifier, and this he undoubtedly was when his achievement is viewed in the context of what appears at least to be the endemic irregularity of so much later Anglo-Norman verse.

LANGUAGE

It is hardly to be expected that, in the fifty or so years that elapsed between the Norman Conquest and the composition of our poem, insular French such as that used by Benedeit should have come to differ at all significantly from its Continental stock. Indeed, it is questionable whether at this early date Anglo-Norman in the sense of a separate vernacular or dialect can be said already to have existed. None the less, Benedeit's text does prove to possess certain linguistic characteristics which it is useful and necessary to describe. Despite the lack of contemporaneous Continental texts for direct comparison, such a description becomes possible on a comparative basis if we use knowledge of later linguistic developments, including those in Anglo-Norman, and postulate a 'standard' Old French literary language for the first half of the twelfth century. This will enable us to isolate certain syntactic and morphological features of Benedeit's French, and at the same time bring to light a number of other characteristics which will fall into two categories: authorial or scribal. These need to be carefully distinguished: on the one hand there are the actual pronunciation habits of the author in so far as these can be reconstructed from the rhymes which he uses (phonology), and on the other the spelling system in our base Ms. (orthography).[23]

Orthography
The use of orthographic conventions in medieval French is neither uniform from text to text nor even necessarily consistent within the

same text, and in this respect the sometimes disconcerting spelling habits of our scribe are not altogether exceptional. He will, for example, on the one hand conform to the Continental practice of spelling the reflex of Latin FIDEM as *fei* 116, while on the other using three variant forms *fai* 70, 298, *feid* 806, 1673, and *fait* 954. His text in fact mixes archaic forms from the first half of the twelfth century with spellings which reflect developments which had come about by the late thirteenth or early fourteenth century when he was writing. Thus in all probability the *t* of *fait* reflects the [θ] sound proper to an early twelfth-century pronunciation, while the *ai* indicates the later Anglo-Norman reduction of the original [ej] dipthong to [ɛ] (to which [aj] had already been levelled). The following is a selection of the more note-worthy insular graphies employed by our scribe which appear in our edited text. Each is accompanied—in brackets—by its 'standard' Continental counterpart for easier identification. The full range of such orthographic variants will be found classified in the Glossary.

a	reparat 823 (repairat), samadi 405 (samedi), chanud 825 (chenu), annüus 972 (enoious)
e	tres 35 (treis), melz 1171 (mielz), le 157 (la), checun 297 (chascun), prestrent 302 (pristrent)
i	primers 1003 (premiers), festïer 842 (festeier)
o	os 636 (ues), soürs 116 (seürs)
u	flur 96 (flour), fus 907 (feus), sun 995 (suen), cruz 675 (croiz), punt 331 (point), cunduz 378 (conduiz), mustrast 49 (mostrast), sulunc 227 (selonc), süurance 121 (seürance)
ai	quai 1256 (quei), paint 760 (peint)
ea	iceals 28 (icels)
ei	malsfeiz 1167 (malsfez), meis 370 (mais), ceil 520 (ciel), oiseil 519 (oisel), suvereins 562 (souverains), veint 211 (vient), bein 34 (bien), peinible 790 (penible)
eo	seons 116 (suens), eols 68 (els)
eu	leus 35 (lieus)
iu	liu 91 (lieu)
oe	iloec 126 (iluec)
oi	oi 393 (hui)
ou	pout 245 (puet), fou 466 (feu)
ui	tuisun 388 (toison)
c	ci 142 (si), castel 267 (chastel), cose 503 (chose), iloces 1363 (ilueques)

cc	secc 968 (sec), peccét 57 (pechié)
ch	chi 857 (qui), unches 500 (onques), drechet 204 (drece)
ck	unckes 1568 (onques)
d	freid 1391 (freit), nud 1222 (nu), vedue 493 (veüe)
g	goie 689 (joie)
k	ki 24 (qui)
n	muntaine 1698 (montaigne)
ng	prengent 629 (prenent)
qu	quer 46 (car)
s	dist 147 (dit), veis 423 (veiz), merveillés 472 (merveilliez)
t	salüet 7 (salüe), mercit 338 (merci)
th	abéth 13 (abé), vetheir 55 (vëeir)
z	blanz 410 (blans)

The spelling of a number of words shows Latin influence, e.g. *Espirit* 131, *angeles* 100, *diviset* 1773, *Naël* 618, *vestiment* 681, and also perhaps *Donna* 1. Preflexional consonants are sometimes restored: *vifs* 45 (*vis*), *colps* 937, *blancs* 499. Final *-s* is lost from the enclitic form *as*: *a* 806, 1324, and from *fors*: *for* 698, final *t* from *dunt*: *dun* 52. There is a tendency also for unstressed *e* to be dropped, resulting in both 'phonetic' spellings such as *un aigue* 1457, *trent* 1563 and in spellings that are at variance with pronunciation: *nent* 981 (*nïent*), *suffreiz* 549 (*sofrerez*), *dimaine* 1305 (*dïemaine*), *entré* 1704 (*entree*). At the same time it is occasionally added adventitiously, as in *averez* 227 or *liverat* 603. In *aparceut* 335 (*aperçut*) it is used as part of a *ce* digraph to denote a [ts] pronunciation (cf. also *receut* 347, 354, and Ms. *voices* 557, *duce* 668, *terce* 1498, the two last emended in our text).

Phonology

A study of Benedeit's rhymes reveals few divergencies from the hypothetical Continental standard, though there are a small number sufficiently attested to make them significant:

1. The linking of [u] with what in Continental French would have been [y], e.g. *murs* (< MŪROS) : *flurs* (< FLŌRES) 1699

    (14 exx.; cf. Pope § 1142)[24]

2. The rhyming of [n] with its palatal counterpart [ɲ], e.g. *seignet* (< SĬGNAT) : *peinet* (< PĒNAT) 1251

    (11 exx.; cf. Pope § 1182)

3. The comparable identity of [l] and [λ],
   e.g. *eisil* (< EXILIUM) : *cil* (<*ECCILLE) 559
   (10 exx.; cf. Pope § 1182)
4. The linking of [ējn] with [ãjn] in rhymes with unstressed final *e*,
   e.g. *meindres* (< MINORES) : *graindres* (< GRANDIORES) 1003
   (6 exx.; cf. Pope § 1159)
5. The identity of what in Continental French would have been [ew]
   and [ɛaw], e.g. *eals* (<ÏLLOS : *beals* (<BELLUS) 1627
   (3 exx.; cf. Pope § 1164)
6. The reduction of the triphthong [jɛy] or [jɛw] in *Judus* 1285, *siu*
   1599, and *fius* 1810, each in rhyme with the [iy] or [iw] diphthong of
   piu(s) [25]
   (3 exx.; cf. Pope § 1168)
7. The development of a diphthong from the group [e] + depalatal-
   ised [λ] in *soleil* : *fedeil* 579, *soleil* : *peil* 1755
   (2 exx.; cf. Pope § 1182)
8. The probable shift of [yi] to [ui] or [wi] after [k] in *quire*
   (< COQUĔRE) : *sire* 1573
   (1 ex.; [26] cf. Pope § 1160)
9. To the above features should be added the reduction of the hiatus
   (syneresis) in certain preterite and impf. subj. forms such as *sousum*
   : *ousum* 763, and the loss of atonic *e* in some futures.[27]

Parts of the etymological impf. indic. of *estre* are admitted in rhymes
with [ē] from tonic free A (86, 1642 etc.), though elsewhere this [ē]
rhymes only with itself. *Sel* < SALEM appears once as *sal* in rhyme with
aval 1340, but this is to be regarded as an exceptional licence (cf. also
the two examples of suffix *-al* < -ALEM at 576, 1093). Exceptional also
is the apparent rhyming of [e] and [je] in *clarté* : *entailét* 275, which is
probably scribal (cf. Waters p. cxxxvii). The vowels [e] and [ɛ] rhyme
together once in *cerne* (< CĬRCINUM) : *verne* (< *VĔRNA) 869. The
diphthong from A + J seems to reduce to [ɛ] in one instance, *lermes* :
termes 892. There are three examples of [ãn] in rhyme with [ãjn]
involving the name *Brandan* (164, 203, 657), no doubt originally in the
variant form *Brandain*. The nasals [ãn] and [ēn] are consistently kept
distinguished. The diphthong [ej] from tonic free close E is never
confused with [oj]. Words reflecting Latin tonic free ō and ŭ give no
sign of having diphthongised in our text, e.g. *penus* : *nus* 1336. Articu-
lation of final supported nasals is apparently preserved in *jurn* 137,
enfern 1329 etc. Though intervocalic and final dentals are often
maintained in spelling, the rhymes show that they had apparently no
phonetic value, e.g. *veüthes* (< *VIDŪTAS): *nues* (< *NŪBAS) 213, *lei*

(< LĒGEM) : *fei* (< FĪDEM) 69, except in verbal terminations within the
line (see Versification above). There is no confusion between final *s*
and *z* ([s] and [ts]).

Morphology, syntax and vocabulary

Of note from the morphological point of view are a number of analogical formations (guaranteed by rhyme and syllable-count), the early
development of which can be assumed to be a dialectal peculiarity of
Anglo-Norman. For example, analogical *-e* has been added in a
number of cases (19 exx. in all) to adjectives and participles which
etymologically do not have a distinctive feminine form, e.g. *forte* 896
(: *morte*), *grande* 240 (: *vïande*), *curante* 178 etc. To these should be
added two instances of analogical pres. indic. forms: *demaine* 1302, *lie*
1451, and possibly three of analogical pres. subj. forms: *esmaie* 226,
crie 1246, *nie* 1452, each showing the development of a non-
etymological *e* in *-er* verbal terminations at the rhyme. Analogical *-s*,
also found early on the Continent, is added in nom. sing. *peres* 146,
155, 354 (: *freres* obl. pl.), *leres* 334 (: *freres* obl. pl.), and graphically at
least in *maigres* 1023, *aigres* 1024, *faitres* 1676, and in the imparisyl-
labics *fels* 529, 1281, and *grips* 1007, 1023, 1025. Features which are
later seen as characteristic of Western-French verb forms are also
present in our text. These include *-c* endings in the pres. indic. first
pers. sg. *prenc* 1304, *revenc* 1399, the pret. first pers. sg. *vinc* 1428,
1540 etc., and palatals in a dozen forms of the pres. subj. of verbs whose
stem ends in *n* or *r*, e.g. *prengent* 1472 (: *calengent*, the only ex.
guaranteed by rhyme). There are in addition several instances of the
impf. indic. terminations in *-oue*, *-out*, *-ouent*, e.g. *celoue* 1275, *reposout* 321, *aürouent* 1287. Unlike many Western and Anglo-Norman
texts, however, the *Brendan* preserves some instances of the etymological 2nd pl. future ending in *-eiz*, e.g. *freiz* 874 (5 exx. in all, none of
them in rhyme), a feature that persisted later in Central and Eastern
dialects than in the West. Contracted futures are fairly common in our
text: *durat* 362, *menrat* 1599, dialectal *truv(e)rat* 246 (8 exx. in all),
and especially the dialectal future forms of *faire*, e.g. *frat* 367 (10 exx.
in all). There are also contracted impf. subj. forms, e.g. *ousum*
764, *poust* 1652, and preterites, e.g. *oustes* 1117 (10 exx. in all).
The form *voldret* 55 may possibly be a relic of the Latin pluperfect
indicative.

Syntactically Benedeit's rhymes indicate relatively careful observance of the two-case declension system for nouns and adjectives, and

despite a score of cases of non-adherence (e.g. *li clers soleil* (sbj.): *un peil* (obj.) 1755), there is no clear evidence that the system was breaking down to any significant extent. There are several instances of the juxtaposed possessive construction, e.g. *diz l'abét* 806, some showing the more usual order of terms reversed, especially with *Deu*, e.g. *en Deu maneie* 225, *par Deu grace* 989. Examples of unusual sentence word-order are plentiful and seem often to be dictated by the needs of the rhyme, e.g. *Seignur servir bien deit l'um tel* 960. Also to be noted is the frequent use of parataxis, in which the linking conjunction or relative between clauses is dispensed with (see note to l. 59), the use of *nul* with negative force without a supporting verbal *ne* (see note to l. 630), and that of *entrer* as a transitive verb (see note to l. 616). Parallels to *arbre* with feminine gender and to masculine *isle*, *flur*, and *dulur* are to be found elsewhere in Anglo-Norman (see note to l. 489).

Besides showing an unusually pronounced Latin influence, Benedeit's vocabulary is interesting also in that it contains a range of rare and even unique French words. Amongst those not attested in any other medieval French text we may cite *avolst*, *beitrer*, *cisler*, *süaté*, *suduine*, *surpeis*, *sururer*, *umeit*. To these should be added two occurrences of English words, *haspe* 686 and *rap* 461 (see note to l. 686). Further lexical details will be found in Waters's articles in *Modern Language Review* 21 (1926), 390–403, and 22 (1927), 28–43.

We append, with all the many reservations which this sort of exercise calls for, a phonetic transcription of ll. 477–94 of our poem. The aim is to provide readers with an approximate idea of how the text might possibly have sounded in the first half of the twelfth century. No two philologists will agree on exactly what sounds are to be inferred from the spellings, and we offer this reconstruction simply in the hope that it may encourage an awareness and possibly also an appreciation of a much neglected area of medieval poetics. We dispense with the phonological explanations and justifications that such a transcription properly requires, except to point out that [ē] represents the development from Latin tonic free A, that we have assumed that Old French [y] and [ɥ] were here pronounced [u] and [w], and that *c* stands for *ch* in *taceledes* 492, and have adopted a dialectal form for *fuilles* 491 (cf. Pope §§ 554, 1142, 1156).

> [priməs lə fist li rejs divins
> dəvānt trestuts pejsuns marins

kwãnt ɔwt tso dit labəs brãndãn
bjēn aθ kuruθ də mēr (un) grãnt pãn   480
vejənt tɛrrə hawt(ə) e klērə
si kum lur ɔwt dit tsil frērə
vjēnənt i tɔst e arivənt
nə del ejsir nə sɛstʃivənt   484
nə pur awtrə rjēn nə dutənt
majz a tɛrrə la nēf butənt
ãmunt un dwit sēn vunt suēf
e ɔθ kɔrdəs trajənt lur nēf   488
aw tʃjēf dew dwit ɔwt un(ə) arbrə
itãnt blãntʃə kumə marbrə
e ləs fuʌəs mowt sunt lēðəs
də rudʒ(ə) e blãnk tatʃəlēðəs   492
də hawtetsə par vəðuə
muntɔwt larbrə sur la nuə]

THE ANGLO-NORMAN POEM

Abbot of a flourishing order of Irish monks, Brendan requests God to
be allowed to visit Heaven and Hell before he dies (19–70). He first
seeks the advice of the hermit Barintus who describes his own sea-
voyage in search of his godson Mernoc which brought him close to
Paradise (102). With fourteen chosen monks, Brendan arrives at the
coast where they proceed to build a currach of timber and oxhide
(184). As they set out in this craft with forty days' provisions, they are
joined by a further three monks who, according to Brendan's explicit
prediction, are to perish in the course of the journey (208). After
fifteen days of rowing despite favourable winds, the monks' boat is
becalmed, but, placing their trust in God, they are able to continue
rowing for a whole month until their food and strength begin to give
out (240). God then sends winds which bring the voyagers to an island
whose high cliffs force them to search for three days before they can
find a suitable place to land (264). Here they discover a splendid city
with many palaces of marble set with gems, and although it proves to
be uninhabited, there is an abundance of food and drink ready for
them (294). One of the intrusive monks steals a golden goblet, and
when, on the fourth day, they are about to leave, he is carried off by the
Devil (354). With fresh provisions provided by a messenger from God

they set out, and after the best part of a year come to a land where they discover white-fleeced sheep as big as stags (390). The messenger orders them to take one, but immediately directs them to a nearby island where the following day they are to celebrate Easter (434). The monks land, cook their food, and are about to eat when suddenly the island begins to quake. Brendan pulls them back into the boat, calmly explaining that they have been sitting on the back of a giant fish (478). In the next island that they come to, they tow their currach up a river as far as a marble-white tree covered with beautiful birds (500). One addresses Brendan telling him that they are fallen angels; it further predicts that the travellers will not reach Paradise for another six years, and that every year they will return to celebrate Easter on the whale's back (552). The monks praise God and rest until after Whitsun when, with their boat refurbished and loaded with eight months' provisions, they set off for the Isle of Ailbe where they are to celebrate Christmas (618). When they finally arrive, an old man appears and leads the travellers to his abbey where they are shown sumptuous treasures and introduced to the community of twenty-four monks of the order of St Ailbe, who prove to be sustained by divine providence (762). The travellers set sail after three weeks, only to be becalmed in the coagulated sea. They finally come to land exhausted and hungry, refresh themselves at an intoxicating spring, but depart again after only a few days (820). Now they return to the cycle of the previous year, celebrating Easter on the back of the fish and revisiting the island of the bird-angels (882). Setting out after a stay of eight weeks, they are attacked first by fire-breathing sea-serpents and then, after landing briefly to take on provisions, by a griffin which is killed in a sea-battle by a flying dragon (1030). Escorted by a school of sea-monsters attracted by Brendan's joyful songs of praise, their boat arrives at a great pillar of jacinth set in the middle of the ocean and surmounted by an altar of emerald under a golden, jewelled canopy. After three days singing mass, they leave taking with them a crystal chalice (1098). A pall of foul-smelling smoke announces their arrival in the region of Hell, where they are assailed by thunderbolts, flames and molten rock, and by red-hot blades of metal hurled by a monster blacksmith (1160). Leaving behind them the cries of the damned, they come to a smoke-capped mountain where the second of the three supernumerary monks is dragged off by Devils (1202). On a nearby rock they catch sight of a pitiful naked figure lashed on all sides by the waves and crying out for mercy. This is Judas, who describes his unending trial of suffering in his double Hell in full and gruesome detail (1263–462), moving Brendan to tears. A third monk, last of the three latecomers, mysteriously disappears as the proceed on their journey. They land on a mountainous island where they meet Paul the Hermit, who had lived and been providentially fed there for ninety of his 140 years (1592). The end of the seventh year of the monks' odyssey is in sight. They return for the last time to the giant fish for Easter and to the island of birds, then set sail eastwards. After forty days they run into thick cloud, pass through by a narrow channel and emerge, on the fourth day, into Paradise (1668). Behind a vast white wall stretching up into the clouds and set with resplendent jewels, is a mountain of pure gold, on top of which lies the garden of Paradise (1700). They are greeted at the gate by a youthful guide who accompanies them through the fields of delicious, sweet-smelling flowers and fruits, flowing with honey and resounding with angelic song (1781). With this all too brief foretaste of what is to come, Brendan and his companions are turned back. Leaving behind their faithful messenger and the young guide, they embark joyfully, and within three months are home again in Ireland (1813). Brendan eventually dies and returns in spirit *u Deus lui destinat* and where his exemplarily pious life is to lead many thousands more.

Belonging as it does to a genre, the Celtic *immram*, that is alien to the literary traditions of Northern France, Benedeit's *Brendan* stands very much on its own in medieval French literature. Though frequently classified as a hagiographic text, the *Brendan* is not strictly speaking a saint's life. This is not to deny, of course, that it is in essence a didactic, edifying story, portraying allegorically the pilgrimage of the soul through testing, suffering and privation to the ultimate goal of Paradise. It is not simply a religious poem, even, but an ascetic and visionary work as well. But above all, and especially for its medieval secular audience, it was a tale of adventure. Its characters are the pliant playthings of divine will, adventuring into the mysterious world of the unknown, yet guided ultimately by a superior force in which they learn to place unqualified trust and faith. Indeed, it is a story not so much of people as of the marvellous adventures that God's creatures are called upon to undergo. In this unreal world of Christianised Celtic mythology, the human and the individual are in every sense subordinated to the divine. What Benedeit's *Brendan* lacks, therefore, in depth of characterisation and psychological insight (a not altogether anachronistic expectation for a twelfth-century audience that was soon to appreciate the romances of Chrétien de Troyes), it compensates for with a swift, varied and dramatic narrative set against a powerful and consistent moral backcloth. Those in search of 'realism' will not be disappointed to find in its place flights of visionary imagination. It is as much in the poem's narrative structure and the imaginative world of fantasy which it recreates as in its didactic aspect that its literary and artistic achievement is to be sought.

The voyage of discovery provides the framework for a long series of more or less autonomous incidents. These unfold, with rapid economy, in an essentially linear manner, but at the same time a deliberate cyclical dimension is introduced into the narrative by the destiny imposed on the travellers to return in successive years to the island of birds and the whale's back, which become thereby focal points of the story. It is of course significant that the cycle revolves around Easter, the beginning of the Church year, and the number seven has clearly been chosen for its symbolic importance. Numerological interpretation also seems called for elsewhere in the text, such as in the number of Brendan's crew (twice seven), and in the period of forty days' wandering before their boat is allowed to penetrate into Paradise, which cannot fail to recall the period of Christ's temptation.[28]

The numerous adventures befalling the monks are of course given unity not only by the fact that each serves as an *exemplum* in the progressive development of their trust in God, but also by the character of Brendan himself, the serene pilgrim *par excellence* whose unnerving prescience sets him apart from his fellows but whose practical wisdom and humanity prevent him from being a mere exemplary cipher. Further cohesion, and even a modest ingredient of suspense, is introduced by the presence of the three intrusive monks who represent the disruptive power of evil and whose deaths, necessary before the ultimate admission into Paradise is possible, punctuate the narrative with constant reminders of the divine retribution which is the wages of sin. This particular lesson reaches a dramatic climax with the long description of the unending torments inflicted on Judas (much of it Benedeit's own embroidery on his Latin source), which is the only significant interruption in the swiftly moving narrative before the arrival in Paradise. The hermit and monks nourished by divine providence, the splendours of the abbey on the Isle of Ailbe, the successive rescuing of the travellers from ever fiercer natural perils, the recurrent appearance of their guardian angel in the form of a messenger, all are there as equally constant reminders of God's beneficence, and more than amply counterbalance the darker, retributive atmosphere that characterises much of the later part of the story. The final triumph over evil and adversity represented by the monks' admission to the Elysian fields is seen as earning the visitors no more than a glimpse of what awaits them if and when they return there definitively in the spirit. In his cursory treatment of the monks' return home and of Brendan's death, all dispatched in a few lines, Benedeit remains faithful to his source in order not to detract from this edifying climax to the adventure-tale. Its moral message Benedeit had been at pains throughout his poem to consolidate, not only by injecting pious observations of his own making and otherwise embroidering but also by implicitly transforming into a trial of faith what in his original was a quest for adventure undertaken explicitly out of curiosity. A large part of the success of Benedeit's reworking and condensing of his source material lies in the extent to which he has struck a fine and consistent balance between the dramatic and the didactic.

One must be careful, however, not to overrate Benedeit's artistic achievement and to lose sight of the fact that he was above all the translator of a pre-existing work. Nevertheless, comparing his French poem with its Latin source, and leaving aside the numerous abridgements which he made both of integral episodes and of incidental detail,[29] it becomes clear that Benedeit had an eye for vivid, concise description and for the dramatic, and an ear for the striking metaphor. The visual aspect of his imagery is particularly noteworthy: independently of his source Benedeit describes how the travellers 'lose sight of everything save sea and clouds' (213–14); how, as they come to land, 'the sea swirls up from hollows below' (257); he amplifies the magnificence of the uninhabited city 'similar in its regal splendour to an emperor's mighty domain' (269–70) with its 'wall of crystal' (272), 'marble palaces . . . resplendent with gems set in gold' (275–6) and the 'fine and beautiful gold and silver plate' (291–2) within; the messenger who appears on the island of sheep is 'white-haired with youthful eyes' (407); the tree in the paradise of birds is 'as white as marble with wide leaves speckled with red and white, and stretching up into the cloud' (490–3); on the Isle of Ailbe Benedeit has the abbot bring out his relics and treasures for his visitors: 'crosses and reliquaries and gospel-books studded with amethysts, adorned with gold and whole precious stones, censers of solid gold set with jewels. The vestments are all of gold, deeper yellow than any in Araby, with huge whole jacinths and sards, their clasps shining with topaz and jasper . . .' (675–86); the sea becomes 'sluggish and dead, making it difficult to sail' (895–6); Paul the Hermit has 'an angelic countenance' (1531), and his island enjoys 'a fine climate, a perpetual summer' (1554); blazing metal falls into the sea and 'there it burns like heather in a woodland clearing' (1157–8). The description (1079–85) of the altar on the blue jacinth pillar rising from the waves (in the original it was of clearest crystal, and no doubt ultimately an iceberg), that of the stench emanating from the volcanic island (1103–10), the hail of molten rock (1123–30), and certain features of the giant blacksmith (1133–42) are all of Benedeit's own invention. These, together with the lurid details of Judas's torments (1353–426), the pathetic account of his misdeeds and suffering (1235–48, 1265–300), both again independent of the Latin *Navigatio*, as well as the greater part of the physical description of Paradise (1669–794) in which Benedeit adapts the pagan vision of the Celtic promised land to an essentially Biblical tradition, can leave the reader in no doubt as to the Anglo-Norman poet's gift for visual description.

In addition to this sort of descriptive embroidery, Benedeit also introduces incidental touches of realistic detail: Brendan throws ropes to the sinking monks on the whale's back, and their clothes are drenched as they scramble back into the ship (459–61); the currach is renovated in preparation for the second year's wanderings (595–600); a sumptuous procession is arranged to welcome the visitors to the Isle of Ailbe (575–90), and monks read aloud in the course of the meal there (698); the travellers moor the boat with chains on the island of birds (865). Other embellishments have the function of dramatising the narrative: the old man on the Isle of Ailbe is 'tall and comes running up to the travellers. They would have been afraid had it not been for the monk's habit that he was wearing' (654–6); the talking bird 'circles all around' (869) before landing on the yard-arm of the boat. The appearance of the first sea-serpent is vividly theatrical: 'the blood in the monks' veins runs cold and they are terribly afraid, for their boat is pitching violently, and because of the storm it is touch-and-go whether it will capsize with them in it. . . . The fire from the sea-serpent flares up like wood in a furnace. The flame is huge and burning hot, and they fear for their lives. The monster's body is unbelievably huge and it bellows louder than fifteen bulls. Even if the only danger had been from its teeth, one thousand and five hundred men would have fled before it. The waves which it caused would alone have made a great storm' (898–915). The graphic scene which follows of the battle between the two serpents (933–52) also springs almost entirely from Benedeit's imagination, as does that of the combat of the griffin and the dragon (1019–26). To Benedeit's skill, therefore, in adapting and condensing his Latin original, in making it both concise and coherent, and in infusing it with a sense of moral direction, is to be added a real capacity for visual and dramatic description which does much to give variety, pace and spice to the narrative.

Passing from the poem's inherent qualities to its place in a broader literary context, it could be argued that, if viewed as a foretaste (albeit Christianised) of the Celtic marvellous that was, a generation or so later, to be so masterfully integrated into the romances of secular, chivalric adventure by Chrétien de Troyes and prove so popular throughout Europe, the Anglo-Norman *Brendan* occupies a more significant position in the development of medieval French literature than it is usually granted. Whether it could also be argued that here, as in other areas (such as Geoffrey of Monmouth's *Historia Regum Britanniae* or Gaimar's *Estoire des Engleis*), insular writers and their audiences were in fact in advance, in literary taste, of their Continental neighbours, is even more a matter of opinion.[30] To Benedeit, at all events, must go the credit not only of being the first writer in French to compose an adventure-tale in octosyllabic couplets but also—and more importantly—of being the first vernacular poet to introduce Celtic material into French literature.

ESTABLISHMENT OF THE TEXT

We have endeavoured to give as faithful an edition as is practicable of Ms. *A* (BL Cott. Vesp. B. X(I)), and to reduce editorial intervention to a minimum, except in the conventionally permitted areas of word-division, capitals, punctuation, the regularised use of *i* and *j*, *u* and *v* etc. We have introduced the acute accent to distinguish tonic from atonic *e* before *t*, *th*, *d*, and *s* (e.g. *cumandet* as pres. indic. 3 alongside *cumandét* as past part.; *merveilles* as adverb beside *merveillés* as pl. imperative), the cedilla to distinguish soft from hard *c*, and diaeresis to mark vowels in hiatus within words. The scribe's omissions of elided *e* are indicated by the apostrophe: *nul' hure*. Contractions have been resolved wherever possible in accordance with the scribe's own spelling habits. Our division of the text into paragraphs follows that of the scribe, and we print his large initial letters in bold type.

Our guiding editorial principle has been the necessarily subjective one of facilitating the readers' understanding of the text of the base Ms. *A*. Our emendations bear, therefore, in the first place on dubious grammatical constructions which comparison with the other Mss. of the poem as well as knowledge of medieval French show to be attributable in all likelihood to the scribe. However, even where it happens that the other Mss. preserve, separately or occasionally unanimously, readings which are preferable to those of Ms. *A*, the latter have not been altered provided that they make acceptable grammatical and syntactic sense and do not falsify the meaning. Where necessary, our Notes indicate such variants.

As for the technical details of Benedeit's prosody, these can best be appreciated in Waters's composite text which skilfully restores to the poet's octosyllables what is assumed to be their pristine regularity. We have, for our part, deliberately refrained from correcting metrically faulty lines purely in order to obtain a correct syllable-count, even where this would have involved simple and quite uncontroversial emendations.

Inconsistencies in spelling, characteristic of so much medieval vernacular writing, have been allowed to stand in all cases where the risk to comprehensibility is considered to be small, e.g. where *vient* < VENIT is written *veint* or *vent*, or *dit* < DICTUM is spelt *dist*. *Le* for feminine *la* is left uncorrected. Such spelling variations are outlined in our Introduction, and room for many of them has been found in the Glossary. Elsewhere, when spellings are isolated (e.g. *pusset* for *puisset*) or when they could be misleading morphologically (as *abes* for *abét*) or semantically (as *esteit* for *estét*), they have been regularised, particularly at the rhyme. In these and in all other instances where the letter of the Ms. has been altered editorially, the original rejected reading figures at the foot of the page.

The number in the right-hand margin indicates changes of folio and column in the Ms. Our line numbers, after l. 476, differ from those of Waters who added three couplets from the other Mss., none, in our view, essential to the understanding of the narrative: his numbers are in advance of ours by two between ll. 477 and 846, by four between ll. 847 and 1238, and by six from l. 1239 to the end.

NOTES TO THE INTRODUCTION

1. For further details see C. Selmer, ed. *Navigatio sancti Brendani Abbatis* (South Bend, Indiana, 1959), xvii–xix, and J. Carney's review of Selmer's edition, *Medium Aevum* 32 (1963), 37–44.
2. *VB*: W. H. Heist, ed. *Vitae Sanctorum Hiberniae ex codice Salmanticensi* (Brussels, 1965), 324–31; *NB*: C. Selmer, *ed. cit.* Selmer's critical edition presents a clear and attractive text, though there are some inaccuracies in footnotes and references. It should be read in conjunction with Carney's review, *art. cit.* For a list of the *VB* and *NB* versions and a general orientation to the Brendan legend, see J. F. Kenney, *The Sources for the Early History of Ireland: Ecclesiastical. An Introduction and Guide* (New York, 1929; rev. impr. L. Bieler, New York, 1966), 406–20. This work also provides details, pp. 417–18, of other documentary records of the Brendan legend, including two ninth-century lives of St Malo, a pupil of Brendan. I. Orlandi published the first volume of a new edition of the Latin *NB* at Milan in 1968. The *Navigatio* can be read in English in J. F. Webb's *Lives of the Saints* (Harmondsworth, 1965) and in J. O'Meara's translation (Dolmen Press, Dublin, 1976).
3. Selmer, *op. cit.*, pp. xxvii–xxix; Carney, *art. cit.*, pp. 41–3.
4. The Voyage of Mael Duin, *Revue celtique* 9 (1888), 447–95; The Voyage of Snédgus and Mac Riagla, *RC* 9 (1888), 14–25; The Voyage of Huí Corra, *RC* 14 (1893), 22–69; all three are edited and translated by Whitley Stokes. A more modern edition, but without translations, is that of A. G. Van Hamel, *Imrama* (Dublin, 1941). An edition and study of *Mael Duin* was recently published by H. P. A. Oskamp (Groningen, 1970). Cf. also D. Dumville, '*Echtrae* and *Immram*: some problems of definition' in *Ériu* 27 (1976), 73–94.
5. Kenney, *op. cit.*, pp. 409–10.
6. Carney, *art. cit.*, pp. 40–1; M. Esposito, *Celtica* 5 (1960), 192–206; L. Bieler, *Celtica* 11 (1976), 15–17.
7. Whitley Stokes, ed. *Lives of Saints from the Book of Lismore* (Oxford, 1890), 98–116, trans. 247–61; D. O'Donoghue, *Brendaniana* (Dublin, 1893) (= *VB*6 in Kenney's list); C. Plummer, *Bethada Náem nÉrenn: Lives of Irish Saints* (Oxford. 1922), I. 44–95. trans. II, 44–92 (= *VB*7 in Kenney's list). Plummer also published a short Irish text, *The Twelve Apostles of Ireland* (I, 98–102, trans. II, 93–8) which has elements of both the *VB* and *NB* traditions, but its many particular episodes and details make it difficult to range with either.
8. C. Selmer, 'The Vernacular translations of the *Navigatio Sancti Brendani*: a bibliographical study', *Mediaeval Studies* 18 (1956), 145–57.
9. See W., pp. lxxxi–cv.
10. A. Jubinal, *La Légende latine de saint Brandaines avec une traduction inédite en prose et en poésie romanes* (Paris, 1836), 105–64, edited from BN fr. 1444; A. Hilka, *Drei Erzählungen aus dem didaktischen Epos 'L'Image du Monde'* (*Brandanus—Natura—Secundus*) (Halle, 1928), 1–49; C. Wahlund, *Die altfranzösische Prosaübersetzung von Brendans*

Meerfahrt (Uppsala–Leipzig, 1900); Alphonse Bayot, 'Le Voyage de saint Brendan dans les légendiers français : essai de classement des manuscrits', *Mélanges Charles Moeller* (Louvain, 1914) i, 456–67; C. Wahlund, 'Eine altprovenzalische Prosaübersetzung von Brendans Meerfahrt', *Beiträge zur romanischen und englischen Philologie. Festgabe für Wendelin Förster* (Halle, 1902), 175–98. Cf. H. R. Jauss and E. Köhler, *Grundriss der romanischen Literaturen des Mittelalters*, vi/2 (Heidelberg, 1970), pp. 243–6 (also vi/1, pp. 200–3); Y. G. Lepage in *Scriptorium* 29 (1975), 29 No. 7.

11. The verse translation was edited by E. Martin, *Zeitschrift für deutsches Altherthum* 16 (1873), 289–322, and by P. F. Moran, *Acta Sancti Brendani* (Dublin, 1872), 45–84. The first of the prose translations (referred to by scholars by the siglum *L*) was printed by Waters in his edition of the *Voyage of St Brendan* (Oxford, 1928) *pari passu* with the French text. C. Selmer discovered another translation (noted as *M*) in Codex 256 of the Biblioteca Nacional in Lisbon and printed it with a discussion of the relationship of *M* to *NB*, the Old French Mss. and to *L*, in *Traditio* 13 (1957), 313–44.

12. For excellent bibliographies of Brendan scholarship, see Kenney, *op. cit.*, 406–8 (up to 1929), C. Selmer, *Navigatio ...*, 117–32 (up to 1959). For the apocryphal connections, see Mario Esposito, 'An apocryphal Book of Enoch and Elias as a possible source of the *Navigatio Sancti Brendani*', *Celtica* 5 (1960), 192–206; D. Dumville, 'Biblical apocrypha and the early Irish: a preliminary investigation', *Proceedings of the Royal Irish Academy* vol. 73, section C (1973), 299–338.

13. A great number of works, both scholarly and popular, which deal with the discovery of America make reference to the Brendan legend: Frederick J. Pohl, *Atlantic Crossings before Columbus* (New York, 1961), ch. 3; C. M. Bolland, *They All Discovered America* (New York, 1961), ch. 5; Geoffrey Ashe et al., *The Quest for America* (London, 1971), ch. 1; S. E. Morison, *The European Discovery of America* (New York, 1971), pp. 1–31; Paul H. Chapman, *The Man who led Columbus to America* (Atlanta, 1973). To support the claim that Irishmen, if not Brendan himself, might have reached North America, an English explorer, Timothy Severin, and a crew of four completed a crossing of the Atlantic in May 1977 in a leather currach made according to the description found in the *Navigatio*; see Severin's own account *The Brendan Voyage* (London, New York, Toronto, 1978). For an account of the geography of the *Navigatio* (and hence of Benedeit's poem), see Geoffrey Ashe, *Land to the West* (London, 1962).

14. Ms. *C* of our classification; see p. 7.

15. Cf. W., p. xxv; M. D. Legge, *Anglo-Norman Literature and its Background* (Oxford, 1963), pp. 9–10, 22, 24, 28; U. T. Holmes, 'The Anglo-Norman Rhymed Chronicle' in *Linguistic and Literary Studies in honor of Helmut A. Hatzfeld*, ed. A. S. Crisafulli (Washington D.C., 1964), 231–6.

16. *Medium Aevum* 19 (1950), 64–6.

17. *Studia Neophilologica* 12 (1939), 46–55.

18. B. Schlyter, ed. (Etudes romanes de Lund 4), Lund, 1941, l. 2000; cit. in the *Anglo-Norman Dictionary*, 1 (London, 1977), p. 32. It should also be noted that, as well as being applied to bishops, legates and messengers, the term is attested in medieval Latin (at an unspecified date) as referring to temporary parish priests at Amiens; see W. H. Maigne d'Arnis, *Lexicon ad scriptores mediae et infimae latinitatis* (Paris, 1886), 175, s.v. *apostoli*: "In dioecesi Ambianensi presbyterii qui parochiis curione viduis deserviendis mittebantur".

19. *Revue de Linguistique romane* 31 (1967), 45–8; cf. W., pp. xxvii ff.

20. Waters (p. xxx) and after him Professor M. D. Legge (*Anglo-Norman Literature and its Background* (Oxford, 1963), pp. 8–18; 'La versification anglo-normande au XIIe siècle' in *Mélanges . . . René Crozet* (Poitiers, 1966), 639-43, see the origin of this verse form in medieval Latin metrics. Waters also presumes the octosyllabic line to have been well established by the time the *Brendan* came to be written.

21. Cf. also note to ll. 53–4 below.

22. Waters, *ed. cit.*, p. lvi.

23. Phonetic symbols are enclosed within square brackets, and are those of the International Phonetic Alphabet. We assume a basic knowledge of medieval French such as that provided, for example, in Glanville Price's *The French Language: Present and Past* (London, 1971). For further details on the language of Benedeit, see ch. VIII of Waters's edition.

24. M. K. Pope, *From Latin to Modern French* (2nd ed., Manchester, 1952).

25 On the exact phonetic value of these sounds, see P. Fouché, *Phonétique historique du français*, II (Paris, 1969), pp. 315–16, 329–33. The difficulty is compounded by the confusion in our text of [u] and [y].

26. But cf. note to l. 41 below.

27. Cf. Morphology below. For the isolated rhymes *ruistes : justes* 41, *men : son* 749, *boche : roche* 1213, *quivere : beivre* 1421, see notes to the text.

28. See further J. H. Caulkins, 'Les notations numériques et temporelles dans la Navigation de Saint Brendan' in *Le Moyen Age* 80 (1974), 245–60; cf. also M. Burrell, 'Narrative structures in *Le Voyage de St. Brendan*' in *Peregon* 17 (1977), 3–9; J. Larmat, 'Le réel et l'imaginaire dans . . . Brandan' in *Voyage, quête, pèlerinage dans la littérature et la civilisation médiévales*, Université de Provence: Cahiers du CUER MA: Senefiance 2 (Paris, 1976), pp. 171–82.

29. Cf. Waters's comparison of the French and Latin texts in his ch. v.

30. See M. D. Legge, 'La précocité de la littérature anglo-normande' in *Cahiers de Civilisation Médiévale* 8 (1965), 327–49; cf. also R. R. Bezzola, *Les Origines et la Formation de la littérature courtoise en Occident* (Paris, 1944–63), part 2, II, pp. 391–461, part 3, II, pp. 3–311; A. Bell, 'Gaimar as pioneer' in *Romania* 97 (1976), 462–80.

Short titles and abbreviations

AN	Anglo-Norman
ANTS	Anglo-Norman Text Society
Gdf.	F. Godefroy, *Dictionnaire de l'ancienne langue française* (Paris, 1880–1902)
Horn	*The Romance of Horn by Thomas*, vol. I ed. M. K. Pope (ANTS 9–10, Oxford, 1955); vol. II M. K. Pope and T. B. W. Reid (ANTS 12–13, Oxford, 1964)
L	The Latin prose translation of Benedeit's text reproduced by Waters; cf. W.
M	The Latin prose translation of Benedeit's text edited by C. Selmer, *Traditio* 13 (1957), 313–44
MLR	*Modern Language Review*
Moignet	Gérard Moignet, *Grammaire de l'ancien français* (2nd ed. Paris, 1976)
NB	*Navigatio Sancti Brendani*; cf. Selmer
OED	*Oxford English Dictionary* (Oxford, 1933)
OF	Old French
OP	Old Provençal
Pope	M. K. Pope, *From Latin to Modern French with especial consideration of Anglo-Norman* (2nd ed. Manchester, 1952)
Selmer	Carl Selmer, ed. *Navigatio Sancti Brendani Abbatis* (South Bend, 1959)
TL	Tobler–Lommatzsch, *Altfranzösisches Wörterbuch* (Berlin, 1925–36, Wiesbaden, 1954–)
VB	*Vita Sancti Brendani*
W.	E. G. R. Waters, ed. *The Anglo-Norman Voyage of St. Brendan by Benedeit* (Oxford, 1928; reprint Geneva, 1974). (A further reprint of Waters's text, with a facing translation into modern German, has been published by E. Ruhe (Klassische Texte des romanischen Mittelalters in zweisprachigen Ausgaben: Band 16), Munich, 1977. Translations of Benedeit's poem into modern French have been made by P. Tuffrau (Paris, 1925) and J. Marchand (Paris, 1940).)

The voyage of St Brendan

by

BENEDEIT

Donna Aaliz la reïne,
Par qui valdrat lei divine,
Par qui creistrat lei de terre
4   E remandrat tante guerre
Por les armes Henri lu rei
E par le cunseil qui ert en tei,
Salüet tei mil e mil feiz
8   Li apostoiles danz Benedeiz.
Que comandas ço ad enpris
Secund sun sens e entremis,
En letre mis e en romanz,
12   Esi cum fud li teons cumanz,
De saint Brendan le bon abéth.
Mais tul defent ne seit gabéth
Quant dit que set e fait que peot:
16   Itel servant blasmer n'esteot.
Mais cil qui peot e ne voile,
Dreiz est que cil mult se doile.
Icist seinz Deu fud néd de reis;
20   De naisance fud des Ireis.
Pur ço que fud de regal lin
Puroc entent a noble fin.
Ben sout que l'escripture dit:
24   'Ki de cest mund fuit le delit,
Od Deu de cel tant en avrat
Que plus demander ne savrat.'
Puroc guerpit cist reials eirs
28   Les fals honurs pur iceals veirs.
Dras de moine, pur estre vil
En cest secle cum en eisil,

8 Benediz   10 e *not in A*   17 si qui   24 f. de d.

Prist e l'ordre e les habiz,
32 Puis fud abes par force esliz.
Par art de lui mult i vindrent
Qui a le ordre bein se tindrent.
Tres mil suz lui par divers leus
36 Munies aveit Brandan li pius,
De lui pernanz tuz ensample
Par sa vertud que ert ample.

Li abes Brendan prist en purpens,
40 Cum hom qui ert de mult grant sens,
De granz cunseilz e de rustes,
Cum cil qui ert forment justes,
De Deu prïer ne fereit fin
44 Pur sei e pur trestut sun lin,
E pur les morz e pur les vifs,
Quer a trestuz ert amis.
Mais de une rien li prist talent
48 Dunt Deu prïer prent plus suvent
Que lui mustrast cel paraïs
U Adam fud primes asis,
Icel qui est nostre heritét
52 Dun nus fumes deseritét.
Bien creit qu'ileoc ad grant glorie,
Si cum nus dit veir' estorie,
Mais nepurtant voldret vetheir
56 U il devreit par dreit setheir,
Mais par peccét Adam forfist,
Pur quei e sei e nus fors mist.
Deu en prïet tenablement
60 Cel lui mustret veablement.
Ainz qu'il murget voldreit vetheir
Quel séd li bon devrunt aveir,
Quel lu li mal aveir devrunt,
64 Quel merite il recevrunt.
Enfern prïed vetheir oveoc
E quels peines avrunt ileoc
Icil felun qui par orguil
68 Ici prennent par eols escuil

1b

De guerrëer Deu e la lei;
Ne entre eols nen unt amur ne fai.
Iço dunt lui pris est desir
72   Voldrat Brandans par Deu sentir.
Od sei primes cunseil en prent
Qu'a un Deu serf confés se rent.
Barinz out nun cil ermite;
76   Murs out bons e sainte vitte.
Li fedeilz Deu en bois estout,
Tres cenz moines od lui out;
De lui prendrat conseil e los,
80   De lui voldrat aveir ados.
Cil li mustrat par plusurs diz,
Beals ensamples e bons respiz,
Qu'il vit en mer e en terre
84   Quant son filiol alat querre:
Ço fud Mernoc qui fud frerre
Del liu u cist abes ere,
Mais de ço fud mult voluntif
88   Que fust ailurs e plus sultif.
Par sun abéth e sun parain   *1c*
En mer se mist e nun en vain,
Quer puis devint en itel liu
92   U nuls n'entret fors sul li piu:
Ço fud en mer en un isle
U mals orrez nuls ne cisle,
U fud poüz de cel odur
96   Que en paraïs gettent li flur,
Quer cel isle tant pres en fud,
U sainz Mernoc esteit curud:
De paraïs out la vie
100   E des angeles out l'oïde.
E puis Barinz la le requist
U vit iço qu'a Brandan dist.
Quant ot Brandan la veüe
104   Que cist out la receüe,
De meilz en creit le soen conseil

---

69 gurrer   73 cunseilz   76 saint   82 bons espiz   83 Quil il
89 parin   90 en un evain   97 cel] del   98 sainz] ainz
100 E les a.   102 vint

E plus enprent sun apareil.
De ses munies quatorze eslist,
108 Tuz les meilurs qu'il i vit,
E dit lur ad le soen purpens;
Savrat par eols si ço ert sens.
Quant oïrent iço de lui,
112 Dunc en parlerent dui e dui.
Respundent lui comunalment
Que ço enprist vassalment;
Prïerent l'en ques meint od sei
116 Cum les seons filz soürs en fei.
Ço dist Brandan: 'Pur cel vos di
Que de vos voil ainz estre fi
Que jo d'ici vos en meinge,
120 Al repentir puis m'en prenge.'
Cil promettent süurance
Pur eols ne seit demurance.
Dunc prent le abes iceols esliz,
124 Puis que out oït d'els les diz;
En capitel les ad menez.
Iloec lur dist cum hoem senez:
'Seignurs, ço que penséd avum
128 Cum cel est gref nus nel savum.
Mes prïum Deu que nus enseint,
Par sun plaisir la nus en meint;
E enz el nun al Saint Espirit
132 Juine faimes que la nus guit,
E junum la quarenteine   *1d*
Sur les treis jurs la semaine.'
Dunc n'i ad nul qui se target
136 De ço faire qu'il lur charget.
Ne li abes ne nuit ne jurn
Des ureisuns ne fait tresturn
De ci que Deus li enveiat
140 Le angel del cel qui l'aveiat
De tut l'eire cum il irat;
Enz en sun quer si l'aspirat
Que tres bien veit e certement

---

113 comunament   120 repenter   128 Cum el   132 iuit
137 nen nuit   142 ci

144 Cum Deus voldrat le seon alment.
   Dunc prent cungé a ses freres,
   As quels il ert mult dulz peres,
   E dist lur ad de seon eire
148 Cument a Deu le voleit creire.
   A sun prïur tuz les concreit,
   Dist lui cument guarder les deit.
   Cumandet eals lui obeïr,
152 Cum lur abét mult bien servir.
   Puis les baiset Brandan e vait.
   Plurent trestuit par grant dehait
   Que mener ne volt lur peres
156 Fors quatorze de lur freres.

   Vait s'en Brandan vers le grant mer
   U sout par Deu que dout entrer.
   Unc ne turnat vers sun parent:
160 En plus cher leu aler entent.
   Alat tant quant terre dure;
   Del sujurner ne prist cure.
   Vint al roceit que li vilain
164 Or apelent le Salt Brandan.
   Icil s'estent durement luin
   Sur l'occean si cume un gruign.
   E suz le gruign aveit un port,
168 Par unt la mer receit un gort,
   Mais petiz ert e mult estreits;
   Del derube veneit tut dreiz.
   Altres, ço crei, avant cestui
172 Ne descendit aval cel pui.
   Ci aloeces fist atraire
   Mairen dunt sa nef fist faire:
   Tut dedenz de fust sapin,
176 Defors l'avolst de quir bovin;
   Uindre la fist qu'esculante   *2a*
   Od l'unde fust e curante.
   Ustilz i mist tant cum estout
180 E cume la nef porter en pout.

La guarisun i mist odveoc
Que il aveient portét iloec:
Ne plus que a quarante dis
184   De vïande n'i out enz mis.
Dist as freres: 'Entrez en enz!
Deus graciëz: bons est li venz.'

Entrerent tuit e il aprés.
188   Ast vos ja tres curanz adés,
A haltes voiz Brandan criant
E lor palmes vers lui tendant:
'De ton muster sumes meüd
192   E desque ci t'avum seüd;
Lai nus, abes, a tei entrer
E od tei, donz, par mer errer.'
Il les cunut e sis receit.
196   Qu'en avendrat bien le purveit:
Ço que par Deu le abes purvit
Ne lur celet, ainz lur ad dist:
'Les dous de vus avrat Satan
200   Od Abiron e od Dathan.
Li tierz de vus mult ert temptez,
Mais par Deu ert bien sustenez.'
Quant out ço dist l'abes Brandans,
204   Dunc drechet sus ambes les mains
E Deu prïet escordement
Les seons fetheilz guard de turment.
E puis levet sus la destre,
208   Tuz les signet li sainz prestre.

Drechent le mast, tendent le veil,
Vunt s'en a plain li Deu fetheil.
Le orrez lur veint de l'orïent
212   Quis en meinet vers occident.
Tutes perdent les veüthes
Fors de la mer e des nües.
Pur le bon vent ne s'en feignent,
216   Mais de nager mult se peinent;
E desirent pener lur cors

182 Qui il aveint   187 Entrent   215 seignent

A ço vetheir pur quei vunt fors.
Si cururent par quinze jurs
220 Desque li venz tuz lur fud gurz:
Dunc s'esmaient tuit li frere   *2b*
Pur le vent qui falit ere.
Li abes dunc les amonestet,
224 Que curages unc ne cesset:
'Metez vus en Deu maneie,
E n'i ait nul qui s'esmaie!
Quant averez vent, siglez sulunc;
228 Cum venz n'i ert, nagez idunc!'
As aviruns dunc se metent.
La grace Deu mult regrettent,
Quer ne sevent quel part aler,
232 Ne quels cordes deient aler,
Quel part beitrer, quel part tendre,
Ne u devrunt lur curs prendre.
Un meis sanz vent nagerent tut plein
236 Tuit li frere par nul desdeign.
Tant cum durat lur vitaile,
Pener pourent sanz defaile.
Force perdent e vïande;
240 Puroc ourent poür grande.

Cum lur avient li granz busuinz,
A ses fetheilz Deus n'est luinz:
Puroc ne deit hoem mescreire.
244 Si cil enprent pur Deu eire,
Tant en face cum faire pout;
Deus li truverat ço que lui estout.
Terre veient grande e halte.
248 Li venz lur vient sanz defalte:
Qui de nager erent penét
Sanz tuz travalz la sunt menét.
Mais n'i truvent nul' entrethe
252 U lur nef fust eschipede,
Quer de rocheiz ert aclose
U nul d'eals entrer n'ose.
Halt sunt li pui en l'air tendant,

221 se maient   230 gracez   248 san   252 nif   253 de] li

256   E sur la mer en luin pendant.
       Des creos desuz la mer resort,
       Pur quei peril i at mult fort.
       Amunt aval port i quistrent,
260   E al querre treis jurs mistrent.
       Un port truvent, la se sunt mis,
       Qui fud trenchéd al liois bis,
       Mais n'i unt leu fors de une nef;
264   Cil fud faitiz en le rocheit blef.   2c
       Ferment la nef, eisent s'en tuit,
       Vunt la veie qui bien les duit.
       Dreit les meinet a un castel
268   Qui riches ert e grant e bel
       E resemblout mult regal leu,
       De emperur mult riche feu.
       Entrerent enz dedenz le mur
272   Qui tuz ert faiz de cristal dur.
       Paleiz veient tuz a marbre,
       N'i out maisun faite de arbre;
       Gemmes od l'or funt grant clarté
276   Dun li pareit sunt entailét.
       Mais une rien mult lur desplout,
       Que en la citét hume n'i out.
       Dunc esgardent l'alçur palais,
280   Entrent en enz al num de pais.

       Enz en le palais Brandan se mist
       E sur un banc puis s'asist.
       Fors sul les soens altres n'i vit;
284   Prent a parler, si lur ad dist:
       'Alez querre par cez mesters
       Si rien i at dun est mesters.'
       Alerent cil e truverent
288   Ço que plus dunc desirerent:
       Ço fud sucurs de vïande
       E de beivre plentét grande;
       De or e de argent la vaisele
292   Que forment fud e bone e bele.

257 resurt   266 vei   271 enz denz   279 les gardent; la cur p.
281 ses m.

Quanque voldrent tut a plentét
Trovent iloec u sunt entrét.
Le abes lur dist: 'Portez nus ent!
296 N'en prengez trop, ço vus defent.
E prïez Deu checun pur sei
Que ne mentet vers Deu sa fai.'
Pur ço les volt li abes guarnir
300 Quer bien purvit que ert a venir.
Cil aportent asez cunrei,
E n'en prestrent a nul desrei;
Tant mangerent cum lur plout,
304 E cum idunc lur en estout.
De Deu loër ne se ublïent,
Mais sa merci mult la crïent.
Del herberger pregnent oser;
308 Quant fud l'ure, vunt reposer.

Cum endormit furent trestuit,   *2d*
Ast vos Sathan qui l'un seduit:
Mist l'en talent prendre an emblét
312 De l'or qu'il vit la ensemblét.
L'abes veilout e bien vetheit
Cume dïables celui teneit,
Cume lui tendeit un hanap de or;
316 Plus riche n'i at en un tresor.
Cil levet sus, prendre l'alat,
E en repost tost l'enmalat.
E puis que out fait le larecin,
320 Revint dormir en sun reclin.
Tut vit l'abes u reposout
Cum cil freres par nuit errout.
Pur tenebres ne remaneit:
324 Sanz candeile tut le vetheit,
Quar quant ço Deus li volt mustrer,
Sur ço n'estout cirge alumer.
Treis jurs enters i sujurnerent
328 E puis al quart s'en turnerent.
Brandans lur dist: 'Seignurs, vus pri,

296 prenget   302 En e p.   315 leui   320 Revin dormer
321 Tuit   325 li *not in* A   328 quarte

Ne portez rien od vus d'ici,
Neïs un punt de cest cunrei,
332 N'enteins l'aigue pur nule sei.'
Forment plurant dist as freres:
'Vedez, seignurs, cist est leres.'
Cil aparceut que l'abes sout
336 Del larecin, cument il l'out
Cunuit; a tuz confés se rent,
A pez le abét mercit atent.
Dist lur abes: 'Prïez pur lui;
340 Vus le verrez murrir encui.'
Devant trestuz tuz veables
Eisit criant li dïables:
'Cheles, Brandan, par quel raisun
344 Gettes mei fors de ma maisun?'
Dist al frere ço que il volt,
Mercit li fait e puis l'asolt.
Desque receut cumungement,
348 Veanz trestuz mort le prent.
L'espirit en vait en paraïs
En grant repos u Deus l'at mis.
Al cors firent sepulture,
352 Prïent Deu qu'en prenget cure.   *3a*
Cist fud un des tres freres
Qu'en la nef receut li peres.
Vindrent al port el rivage.
356 Ast vus mult tost un message:
Pain lur portet e le beivre
E sis rovet cel receivre.
Puis lur at dist: 'Soür sëez,
360 Quelque peril que vus veiez.
Que que veiez, n'aëz poür:
Deus vus durat mult bon oür,
E ço verrez que alez querant
364 Par la vertud de Deu le grant.
E de cunrei nen esmaëz
Que vus ici asez n'en aiez:

332 nul se   334 Veidez   336 larcein   338 abes   344 ma *not in* A
345 qui   350 repose   352 que p.   355 Vindrint   358 cil
359 seet

Ne frat faile desqu'en vendrez
368   En tel leu u plus prendrez.'
Parfunt clinant, saisit les en.
Plus ne lur dist, meis alat s'en.

Or unt voüt li Deu servant
372   Que il eirent par Deu cumant,
E unt pruvét tut a soüt
Par miracles que unt voüt.
E bien veient que Deus les paist:
376   De loër Deu nuls ne se taist.
Siglent al vent, vunt s'en adés.
Li cunduz Deu mult lor est pres.
Curent par mer grant part de l'an
380   E merveilles trestrent ahan.
Terre veient a lur espeir,
Cum de plus luin lur pout pareir.
Drechent lur nef icele part,
384   E n'i at nul de nager se tart.
Lascent cordes, metent veil jus;
Ariverent e sailent sus.
Veient berbiz a grant fuisun,
388   A chescune blanche tuisun.
Tutes erent itant grandes
Cum sunt li cers par ces landes.
Dist lur l'abes: 'Seignurs, d'ici
392   Ne nus muverum devant terz di.
Jusdi est oi de la ceine,
Cum li Filz Deu suffrit peine;
Il nus est douz e prest amis
396   Qui prestement nus ad tramis
Dunt poüm la feste faire.   *3b*
Pensez de la nef sus traire!
De icez berbiz une pernez,
400   Al di pascal la cunrëez.
A Deu cungét de ço ruvum,
Altre quant nus or n'i truvum.'

---

367 Nen; dis quen   368 leiu   373 un   375 veiant; le   383 icel
384 de le nager   387 granz   393 Judis 395 e epres   397 fest

Que cumandat, iço fait unt,
404 E par tres dis ileoc estunt.
Al samadi lur vient uns mes,
De la part Deu salüet les.
Peil out chanut, oilz juvenilz:
408 Mult out vescut sanz tuz perilz.
Pain lur portet de sun païs:
Grant e mult blanz guasteus alis;
E si lur falt nule rien,
412 Tut lur truverat, ço promet bien.
L'estre d'iloc l'abes anquist.
Ne sai s'osat, mais poi l'en dist;
Ço respundit: 'Asez avum
416 Quanque des quers penser savum.'
E dist l'abes: 'Berbiz ad ci,
Unc en nul leu tant grant ne vi.'
Respunt lui cil: 'N'est merveille:
420 Ja ci n'ert traite öeile;
L'ivers n'en fait raëncune,
Ne d'enfertét n'i mort une.
A cel isle que tu veis la,
424 Entre en ta nef, Brandan, e va.
En cel isle anuit entras
E ta feste demain i fras.
Demain enz nuit en turnerez;
428 Pur quei si tost, bien le verrez!
Puis revendrez e sanz peril,
Bien pres siglant de cest costil.
E puis irez en altre liu
432 U jo en vois e la vus siu.
Mult pres d'ici, la vus truverai;
Asez cunrei vus porterai.'

Siglet Brandan, nel cuntredit;
436 Vait a l'isle que il bien vit.
Vent out par Deu e tost i fud,
Mais bien grant mer out trescurud;
Eissi vait qui Deus maine.
440 Terre prennent e sanz peine.
414 soasat

Eissent s'en fors tuit li frere
Fors sul l'abes qui enz ere.
Beal servise e mult entrin
444   Firent la nuit e le matin.
Puis que unt tut fait lur servise
En la nef cum en eglise,
Charn de la nef qu'il i mistrent,
448   Pur quire la dunc la pristrent.
De la busche en vunt quere
Dunt le manger funt a terre.
Cum li mangers fud cunrëez,
452   Dist li bailis: 'Or asëez!'
Dunc s'escrïent mult haltement:
'A! donz abes, quar nus atent!'
Quar la terre tute muveit
456   E de la nef mult se luigneit.
Dist li abes: 'Ne vus tamez,
Mais Damnedeu mult reclamez!
E pernez tut nostre cunrei,
460   Enz en la nef venez a mei!'
Jetet lur fuz e bien luncs raps;
Parmi tut ço muilent lur dras.
Enz en la nef entré sunt tuit.
464   Mais lur isle mult tost s'en fuit,
E de dis liuues bien choisirent
Le fou sur lui qu'il i firent.
Brandan lur dist: 'Freres, savez
468   Pur quei poür oüt avez?
N'est pas terre, ainz est beste
U nus feïmes nostre feste,
Pessuns de mer sur les greinurs.
472   Ne merveillés de ço, seignurs!
Pur ço vus volt Deus ci mener
Que il vus voleit plus asener:
Ses merveilles cum plus verrez,
476   En lui puis mult mielz crerrez.
Primes le fist li reis divins
Devant trestuz pessuns marins.'

442 en ere   443 sevise   445 out   446 glise   453 ses scirent
465 luiues; chosserent   474 Qui

Quant out ço dist l'abes Brandan,
480 Bien ad curut de mer un grant pan.
Veient terre alte e clere,
Si cum lur out dist cil frere.
Venent i tost e arivent,
484 Ne de l'eisir ne s'eschivent,
Ne pur altre rien ne dutent,   *3d*
Mais a terre la nef butent.
Amunt un duit s'en vunt süef
488 E od cordes traient lur nef.
Al chef del duit out une arbre
Itant blanche cume marbre,
E les fuiles mult sunt ledes,
492 De ruge e blanc taceledes.
De haltece par vedue
Muntout le arbre sur la nue;
Des le sumét desque en terre
496 La brancheie mult la serre
E ledement s'estent par l'air,
Umbraiet luin e tolt le clair;
Tute asise de blancs oiseus:
500 Unches nul hom ne vit tant beus.

Li abes prent a merveiller
E prïet Deu sun conseller
Que li mustret quel cose seit,
504 Si grant plentét des oiseus que deit,
Quel leu ço seit u est venuz;
D'iço l'asent par ses vertuz.
Sa prïere quant la laisat,
508 L'un des oiseus s'en devolat.
Tant dulcement sonat li vols
En eschele cum fait li cols;
E puis qu'asist desur la nef,
512 Brandan parlat bel e süef:
'Si tu es de Deu creature,
De mes diz dunc prenges cure!
Primes me di que tu seies,

481 a. edere   482 Cil cum   484 ne se sivent   492 e *not in* A
503 Qui   513 crature   514 meis

516   En cest liu que tu deies,
        E tu e tuit li altre oisel,
        Pur ço que a mei semblez mult bel.'
        L'oiseil respunt: 'Angele sumes,
520   E enz en ceil jadis fumes;
        E chaïmes de halt si bas
        Od l'orguillus e od le las
        Par superbe qui revelat,
524   Vers sun seignur mal s'eslevat.
        Cil fut sur nus mis a meistre,
        De vertuz Deu nus dut paistre;
        Puroc que fu de grant saveir,
528   Sil nus estout a meistre aveir.
        Cil fud mult fels par superbe,   *4a*
        En desdein prist la Deu verbe.
        Puis que out ço fait, lui servimes
532   E cum anceis obedimes;
        Pur ço sumes deseritét
        De cel regne de veritét.
        Mais quant iço par nus ne fud,
536   Tant en avum par Deu vertud:
        N'avum peine si cum cil
        Qui menerent orguil cum il.
        Mal nen avum fors sul itant:
540   La majestéd sumes perdant,
        La presence de la glorie,
        E devant Deu la baldorie.
        Le num del leu que tu quesis,
544   C'est as Oiseus li Paraïs.'
        E il lur dist: 'Or ad un an
        Que avez suffert de mer le han;
        Arere sunt uncore sis
548   Ainz que vengez en paraïs.
        Mult suffreiz e peines e mal
        Par occean, amunt aval,
        E chescun an i frez la feste
552   De la Pasche sur la beste.'

523 que relvelat   524 les lavat   528 Si   530 En desclem
538 manerent   545 il *not in* A   547 seis   548 Anz   550 amult
551 C ch.

Puis que out ço dist, si s'en alat
En sun arbre dun devalat.
Quant vint le jurn al declinant,
556 Vers le vespre dunc funt cant;
Od dulces voices mult halt crïent
E enz en le cant Deu mercïent.
Or unt veüd en lur eisil
560 Itel cumfort cum urent cil.
Humaine gent unches anceis
N'i enveiat li suvereins reis.
Dunc dist le abes: 'Avez oïd
564 Cum cist angele nus unt goïd?
Loëz Deu e gracïez,
Plus vus aimet que ne quïez!'
La nef leisent en l'ewage
568 E mangerent al rivage;
E puis chantent la cumplie
Od mult grant psalmodie.
Puis enz as liz tuit s'espandent
572 E a Jesu se cumandent.
Dorment cum cil qui sunt lassét   *4b*
E tanz perilz qui unt passét.
Mais nepurtant a chant de gals
576 Matines dïent ainzjurnals,
E as refreiz ensemble od eals
Respunt li cors de cez oisals.

En prime main al cler soleil
580 Ast vus venant le Deu fedeil
Par qui asen unt cest avei,
E par sun dun unt le cunrei.
E il lur ad dist: 'De vïande
584 Jo vus truverai plentét grande;
Asez averez e sanz custe
As uitaves de Pentecuste.
Puis les travalz estout sujurn:
588 Dous meis estrez ci enturn.'
Dunc prent cungé e s'en alat,

553 Pui   557 creient   561 a ceis   567 en leugue   577 od] ed
580 le] de   587 en jurn

E al terz di la repairat.
Dous feiz tuz dis la semaine
592 Cil revisdout la cumpaine.
Cum lur ad dist, eissil firent,
En sun seign tut se mistrent.
Quant vint li tens de lur errer,
596 Lur nef prengent dunc a serrer;
De quirs de buf la purcusent,
Quar cil qu'i sunt a plein usent;
Asez en unt a remüers
600 Que estre puisset lur baz enters.
E bien de tut se guarnissent
Pur defalte ne perisent.
Cil lur liverat pain e beivre
604 Cum il voldrent plus receivre.
Tut ad cunté a pleins uit meis;
La nef ne pout plus suffrir peis.
Quant cil e cil baisét s'en sunt,
608 Prengnent cungét e puis s'en vunt.
Cil lur mustrat od mult grant plurs
Quel part dourent tendre lur curs.
Ast vus l'oisel desur le mast:
612 Dist a Brandan que s'en alast.
Granz curs li dist qu'ad a faire,
E mult ennois ad a traire:
Uit meis enters estreit baïs
616 Ainz que puisset entrer païs,
Ainz qu'a l'isle vengent Albeu   *4c*
U estreient al Naël Deu.
Puis qu'out ço dist, plus n'i targe;
620 Vait s'en al vent tut la barge.

Vunt s'en mult tost en mer siglant,
De tant bon vent Deu graciant.
Crut lur li venz e mult suvent
624 Crement peril e grant turment.
Puis quatre meis veient terre,

594 seig   598 que s.   599 e r.   601 guarnisseint
602 periseint   610 Que p.   612 alat   613 succurs   616 pusset
617 ad i.; abeu   618 estreint

Mais fort lur est a cunquerre.
E nepurtant a la parfin
628 Al siste meis virent la fin.
Prengent terre, mais nepuroec
Nul' entree truvent iloec.
Virun en vunt .xl. dis
632 Ainz que en nul port se seient mis,
Quar li rocheit e li munz grant
A la terre lur sunt devant.
Puis mult a tart truvent un cros
636 Que fait uns duiz, qui lur ad os.
Qui cundüent lur nef amunt
Reposent sei quar lassét sunt.
Puis dist l'abes: 'Eisums fors;
640 Querums que seit mester as cors.'
Eisent s'en tuit uns e uns,
L'abes ovoec ses cumpaignuns;
E funtaine trovent duble,
644 L'une clere, l'autre truble.
Vunt i curant cum sedeillus.
Dist lur l'abes: 'Retenez vus!
Prendre si tost jo vus defent
648 D'ici que avum parlé od gent.
Quel nature nus ne savum
Aient li duit que trovét avum.'
Les diz l'abét, cil les crement,
652 E lur mult grant seif, le prement.
Hastivement e nun a tart,
Ast vus currant un grant veilard.
Poür oussent ne fust l'abit,
656 Quar moines ert; mais rien ne dit.
Vient enchaër as pez Brandan.
Drechet lui sus cil par la main.
Clinet parfunt e humlement;
660 Le abét e tuz baiser enprent.
Puis prent Brandan par la destre
Pur mener l'en a sun estre.
As altres dist par sun seigne

4d

628 meis iurn la f.   629 a t.; que pur oec   649 nel   651 labes
652 les p.   660 abes e tuit

664   Vengent vedeir leu mult digne.
       Cume alouent, le abes ad quis
       Quels leus ço seit u se sunt mis.
       Mais cil se taist, respuns ne fait;
668   Goït les fort od mult dulz hait.
       Tant unt alét que ore veient
       Le leu u il aler deient:
       Abeïe bele e bone;
672   Plus sainte n'at suth le trone.
       Le abes del leu fait porter fors
       Ses reliques e ses tresors:
       Cruz e fertres e les tistes,
676   Bien engemmét de amestistes,
       De or adubez e de peres
       Precïuses e enteres,
       Od encensers de or amassét
680   E les gemmes enz encassét.
       Li vestiment sunt tuit a or;
       En Arabie nen at si sor;
       Od jagunces e sardines
684   Forment grandes e entrines;
       Od tupazes e od les jaspes
       Itant clers sunt les haspes.
       Tuit li moine sunt revestud,
688   Od lur abét sunt fors eisud.
       Od grant goie e grant dulceur
       Processïun funt li seignur.
       E quant baisét se sunt trestuit,
692   Chescun le altre par la main duit.
       Meinent les en lur abeïe,
       Brandan e sa cumpainie.
       Servise funt bel e leger;
696   Nel voleient trop agreger.
       Puis vunt manger en refraitur
       U tuit taisent fors li litur.
       Devant eals unt dulz e blanc pain
700   Bien savurét e forment sain.
       Racines unt en lu de mes,

668 duce   679 censers *expuncted* encers   688 abes   697 fraitur
698 for   699 dulce

Qui sur deintez saülent les.
Puis unt beivre mult savurét:
704   Aigue dulce plus de murét.
Quant sunt refait, levét s'en sunt   5a
E verseilant al muster vunt.
Vunt verseilant miserere
708   Desque en estals tuit li frere
Fors iceals qui servirent;
En refreitur cil resirent.
Quant l'eschele fud sonee,
712   Puis que l'ure fud chantee,
L'abes del leu fors les meinet.
D'els e del leu lur enseignet:
Qui sunt, cument, des quant i sunt,
716   De qui, par qui succurs unt:
'Nus sumes ci vint e .iiii.;
Ci conversum en cest atre.
Uitante anz ad que prist sa fin
720   Saint Albeu li pelerin.
Riches hom fud de mult grant fiu,
Mais tut guerpit pur cest leu.
Quant alat en tapinage,
724   Apparut lui Deu message
Qui l'amenat; trovat leu prest:
Icest muster que uncore i est.
Quant oïmes en plusurs leus
728   Que ci maneit Albeus li pius,
Par Deu ci nus asemblames
Pur lui que nus mult amames.
Tant cum vesquit, lui servimes,
732   Cume a abét obeïmes.
Puis que le ordre nus out apris
E fermement nus out asis,
Dunc lui prist Deus de sei pres;
736   Uitante anz ad que prist decés.
Deus nus ad puis si sustenuz
Que nuls mals n'est sur nus venuz,

702 saluent   703 mul   711 sone   512 chante   714 de leu
715 Si sunt   716 sunt   720 A saint A.; pelerein   722 tuit
725 amanat   732 abes   737 ad *not in* A

De nostre cors nul' enfermetét,
740 Ne peisance ne amertét.
De Deus nus veint, el ne savum,
La vïande que nus avum.
Nus n'i avum nul loreür,
744 Ne n'i veduns aporteür,
Mais chescun jurn tut prest trovum,
Sanz ço qu'ailur nus nel ruvum,
Tute veie le jurn uvrer
748 Entre les dous un pain enter;
A di festal ai tut le men   *5b*
Pur le super, e chascun le son.
E des dous duiz que veïstes,
752 Dunt pur un poi ne preïstes,
Li clers est freiz que al beivre avum,
Li trubles calz dun nus lavum.
E as hures que nus devum
756 En noz lampes fou recevum,
Ne pur l'arsun que cist fous fait
Cire ne oile le plus n'en vait;
Par lui emprent, par lui esteint,
760 N'avum frere de ço se paint.
Ici vivum e sanz cure,
Nule vie n'avum dure.
Ainz que vostre venir sousum,
764 Volt Deus qu'a vus cunrei ousum.
Il le dublat plus que ne solt;
Bien sai que vus receivre volt.
Des Thephanie al uitime di
768 Dunc a primes muverez d'ici;
Desque dunches sujurnerez,
Puis a primes vus an irez.
Dunc dist Brandans: 'N'est liu si chers
772 U mansisse si volunters.'
Respunt l'abes: 'Ço va quere
Pur quei moüs de ta terre,
Puis revendras en tun païs,

741 veïent   744 venduns   745 tuit   746 nus] nes   747 vie
753 Li cres   755 Ehas   765 le *not in* A   766 vus refaire v.
767 thepanie   772 mansesisse

776 Ileoc muras u tu nasquis.
    Muveras d'ici la semaine
    As uitaves de Thephaine.'

    Quant vint le jurn que l'abes mist,
780 Brandan de lui le cungé prist;
    Li uns abes l'altre cunduit,
    Ensemble od lui li moine tuit.
    Entrent en mer, vent unt par Deu
784 Qui les luinet de l'isle Albeu.
    Curent en mer par mult lunc tens,
    Mais de terre unt nul asens.
    Failent al vent e a cunreid;
788 Crut l'egre faim e l'ardant seid;
    E la mer fud tant paisible
    Pur quei unt le curs mult peinible.
    Espesse fud cume palud;
792 Tel i out enz ne creit salud.
    Deus les succurt par orage: *5c*
    Terre veient e rivage,
    E bien sevent li afamét
796 Que la les ad Deus destinét.
    Trovent tel lur entree
    Cume se lur fust destinee.
    Un duit unt cler e pessuns denz,
800 E cil em prenent plus que cenz.
    Mester lur unt virun l'umeit
    Herbes que sunt en betumeit.
    L'abes lur dist: 'N'aiez cure
804 De beivre trop sanz mesure.'
    Cil em pristrent secund lur seid,
    A diz l'abét ne tenent feid.
    Tant em pristrent puis a celét
808 Pur quei furent fol apelét,
    Quar li sumnes lur cureit sus
    Dum il dormant giseient jus.
    Qui trop beveit giseit enclins,

779 veint   780 leu   786 sens   789 passibile   791 palude
792 salude   801 virun *not in A*   804 De *not in A*   806 diz abet
807 alelet   809 curent   811 geisent

812   Tel jurn, tel dous, tel .iii. entrins.
      Brandan prïout pur ses muines
      Que il vedeit tuz suduines.
      Desqu'en lur sens cil revindrent,
816   Pur fols forment tuit se tindrent.
      Dist lur abes: 'Fuium d'ici
      Que ne chaiez meis en ubli.
      Mielz vient suffrir honeste faim
820   Que ublïer Deu e sun reclaim.'
      Par mer d'ileoc se sunt tolud,
      Desque al jusdi vint absolud;
      Dunc reparat peres Brandan
824   En la terre u fud l'altre an.
      Ast lur hoste, le veil chanud:
      Al port lur ad un tref tendud;
      Bainéd i ad les travailez,
828   E nuveals dras apareilez.
      Funt la ceine e lur mandét
      Cum en escrit est cumandét.
      E sunt ileoc desque al .iii. di.
832   Turnerent s'en al samadi
      E vunt siglant sur le peisun.
      L'abes lur dist: 'Fors eisum!'
      Lur caldere qu'il perdirent
836   En l'an devant, or la virent;
      Li jacoines l'ad gwardee,   *5d*
      Or l'unt sur lui retruvee.
      Plus asoür sur lui estunt,
840   E lur feste bele i funt.
      Tute la nuit desque al matin
      De festïer ne firent fin.
      Le di paschur celebrïent;
844   De lur hure ne s'ublïent:
      Plus de midi ne targerent,
      Mais dunc lur nef rechargerent.
      Alat s'en tost e curt li sainz
848   Vers les oiseus u furent ainz.
      Bien unt choisit le arbre blanche

814 il ne deit tuit   815 Desque lur   818 umbli   826 porte
838 Or unt   839 Pluis   841 Tut   843 celebreient   849 un

E les oiseals sur la branche.
De luin en mer bien oïrent
852 Cum li oiseals les goïrent:
De lur canter ne firent fin
Desque arivé sunt li pelerin.
Traient lur nef amunt le gort
856 La u devant ourent lur port.
Ast lur hoste chi tent un tref:
Cunreid portet pleine sa nef.
Dist lur: 'Ci streiz del tens un poi.
860 A voz cungez jo m'en revoi.
Ici mandrez e sanz custe
Desque uitaves de Pentecoste.
Ne dutez rien; ne demurai:
864 Quant mesters ert, vus succurrai.'
Ferment lur nef od chaines,
E sunt iloec set semaines.
Quant vint le tens de lur aler,
868 L'un des oiseals prent avaler:
Sun vol ad fait tut a cerne,
Puis s'est asis sur la verne.
Parler voldrat; Brandan le veit,
872 Dist a checun que em pais seit:
'Seignurs', ço dist, 'a cest sujurn
Tuz cez set anz freiz vostre turn.
Chascun an al Naël Deu
876 Sujurnerez en l'isle Albeu;
La ceine freiz e le mandét
U vostre hoste l'at cumandét.
E chescun an freiz la feste
880 De la Pasche sur la beste.'
Quant out ço dist, si s'en alat   *6a*
En sun arbre dum devolat.
La nef en mer parfunt flotet;
884 L'oste chescuns aböotet.
Chil de venir ne s'est targét:
Vent de cunrei sun bat chargét,
E de sa nef charget la lur

---

851 oierent   852 goierent   853 fin *not in A*   856 U la   859 streit
869 uols   874 set *not in A*   876 en isle   887 la *not in A*

888 Od bon cunrei de grant valur.
Puis apelet Filz Marie
Qui guart cele cumpainie.
Del revenir metent termes.
892 Al departir fundent lermes.

Trestout curent al portant vent
Chi fait errer vers occident.
Dormante mer unt e morte
896 Chi a sigler lur ert forte.
Puis q'unt curut .iii. quinzeines,
Freidur lur curt par les veines:
Poür lur surt forment grande
900 Que lur nef est tut en brande,
E poi en falt pur turmente
La nef od eals que n'adente.
Puis lur veint el dun s'esmaient
904 Plus que pur nul mal qu'il traient:
Vers eals veint uns marins serpenz
Chi enchaced plus tost que venz.
Li fus de lui si enbraise
908 Cume buche de fornaise:
La flamme est grant, escalféd fort,
Pur quei icil crement la mort.
Sanz mesure grant ad le cors;
912 Plus halt braiet que quinze tors.
Peril n'i oust fors sul de denz,
Sil fuïssent mil e cinc cenz.
Sur les undes que il muveit,
916 Pur grant turment plus n'estuveit.
Cum aprismout les pelerins,
Dunc dist Brandan li veirs divins:
'Seignurs, n'entrez en dutance:
920 Deus vus ferat la venjance.
Guardez que pur fole poür
Deu ne perdez ne bon oür,
Quar que Deus prent en sun cunduit
924 Ne deit cremer beste qui muit.'

890 cel (*or* tel?)   903 v. e d.   909 La flum   913 out
914 Cil furent   915 qui il

Puis que out dist, a Deu urat;   *6b*
Ço qu'out urét ne demurat:
Altre beste veient venir
928 Qui bien le deit cuntretenir.
Dreit cum ceste vers la nef traist,
L'altre qui vient a rage braist.
Ceste cunuit sa guarrere;
932 Guerpit la nef, traist s'arere.
Justedes sunt les dous bestes:
Drechent forment halt les testes;
Des narines li fous lur salt,
936 Desque as nües qui volet halt.
Colps se dunent de lur noës,
Tels cum escuz, e des podes.
A denz mordanz se nafrerent,
940 Qui cum espiez trenchant erent.
Salt ent li sanz des aigres mors
Que funt li denz en cez granz cors;
Les plaies sunt mult parfundes,
944 Dun senglantes sunt les undes.
La bataile fud estulte:
En la mer out grant tumulte.
E puis venquit la dereine;
948 Morte rent la primereine:
A denz tant fort la detirat
Que en tres meitez le descirat.
E puis que fist la venjance,
952 Realat a sa remanance.

Ne deit hom mais desesperer,
Ainz deit sa fait plus averer
Quant veit que Deus si prestement
956 Vivere trovet e vestement,
E tanz succurs en perilz forz
E estorses de tantes morz.
L'abes lur dist: 'Laisum tut el:
960 Seignur servir bien deit l'um tel.'
Cil respunent mult volunters:

929 cest   930 veient arge   931 Cest   932 sairere   940 espiz
941 enz li s. fud a.   953 desperer   958 tante

'Quar bien savum qu'il nus ad chers.'
Puis al demain terre veient,
964 E ariver bien se creient.
Vunt mult tost e sailent fors
Pur reposer lur lassez cors.
Sur l'erbeie tendent lur tref,
968 E sus traient al secc lur nef.
Cum a terre ariverent,   *6c*
Les tempestes aviverent;
Cunuit Brandans a l'air pluius
972 Que li tens ert mult annüus.
Li venz lur ert cuntresailiz,
E li cunreiz lur ert failiz;
Mais cil puroc ne s'esmaient,
976 Quelque peril que il traient.
L'abes lur ad tant sermunét,
E Deus par tut asez dunét,
Que ne poient puint mescreire
980 De nule rien en lur eire.
Puis aprés ço, nent a tart,
Del peisun veint la terce part;
L'unde de mer tant la serre
984 Que ariver lur fait a terre;
La turmente sus la chacet
Pur ço que a cez aise facet.
Dunc dist Brandans: 'Veiez, frere,
988 Ki enemis ainz vos ere
Or nus succurt par Deu grace:
Mangerez en grant espace.
Ne dutez rien, il nus ert past,
992 Quelque semblant qu'il nus mustrast.
Tant en pernez as voz suspeis
Que ne failet devant .iii. meis.'
Al sun cumant cil le firent:
996 A tant de tens se guarnirent.
D'eigue dulce des funtaines
Funt lur tunes tutes pleines,
E de busche se guarnirent.
1000 Puis q'unt l'uré, s'en issirent.

962 qui   982 veient   1000 sen alirent

De miracles Deus ne cesset:
Altre peril les apresset.
Si fust primers, ne fust meindres
1004 Icist perilz, enz fust graindres.
Mais ne crement pur le purpens
Qu'il unt de Deu, e le defens.
Uns grips flammanz de l'air descent,
1008 Pur eals prendre les ungles tent,
E flammantes ad les goës
E trenchantes fort les poës.
Bord de la nef n'i ad si fort
1012 Sul od l'ungle que ne l'en port;
Pur sul l'aïr e le sun vent
Pur poi la nef achant ne prent.
Cum les caçout eisi par mer,
1016 Vint uns draguns flammanz mult cler;
Mot les eles, tent le col,
Vers le gripun drechet sun vol.
La bataile sus est en l'air:
1020 Li fus des dous fait grant esclair;
Colps e flammes e morz e buz
Se entredunent veiant eals tuz.
Li grips est granz, draguns maigres;
1024 Cil est plus fort, cil plus aigres.
Morz est li grips, en mer chaït:
Vengét en sunt ki l'unt haït.
Vait s'en draguns, portet victorie;
1028 Cil en rendent Deu la glorie.
Vunt s'en icil d'iloec avant;
Par l'espirit Deu mult sunt savant.

Vint la feste de saint Perrunt
1032 Ki fud ocis al préd Nerunt;
Feste li funt cil e glorie
A saint Perrunt l'apostorie.
Cum l'abes fist le servise,
1036 Sicum la lei est asise,
Chantout mult halt a voiz clere.

6d

1012 lungles   1014 naf   1016 f. par mer   1020 de dous
1036 Sicum lais

Dunc dïent tuit li frere:
'Beal pere chers, chante plus bas,
1040   U si ço nun, murir nus fras;
Quar tant cler' est chascun' unde
U la mer est parfunde
Que nus veüm desque en terre,
1044   E de peissuns tante guerre.
Peissuns veüm granz e crüels,
Unc n'oïmes parler de tels.
Si la noise les en commout,
1048   Sachez, murir nus estout.'
L'abes surrist e les blasmat,
E pur mult fols les aësmat:
'Seignurs, de rien pur quei dutez?
1052   Voz crëances cum debutez!'
Perilz avez suffert plus granz;
Vers tuz vus fud Deus bons guaranz.
Uncore ne vus vint cist.
1056   Clamez culpe!', Brandans lur dist.
Chantat plus halt e forment cler.   *7a*
Sailent bestes ruistes de mer,
Vunt costeant la nef enturn,
1060   Goïsant la feste del jurn.
Puis q'unt chantét que al jurn partint,
Chescun peissun sa veie tint.

Avant curent e veient cler
1064   En mer halte un grant piler:
De naturel fud jargunce;
D'altre mairein n'i out unce;
De jargunce fud saphire;
1068   Riches estreit ki'n fust sire.
Desqu'as nües muntout en sus,
As funs de mer descendeit jus.
Uns paveiluns enturn i tent;
1072   Des le sumét en mer descent,
De or precïus uvrét sutil:

1040 si que nun murer   1043 venum   1044 gurre   1050 asinat
1052 creance   1059 costant   1063 Quant   1064 halt
1073 il veirent s.

Pur tut le munde faiz ne fust il.
Siglet Brandan icele part;
1076 Ainz que venget semblet lui tart.
Sigle levét entret en tref
Od ses muines e od sa nef.
D'esmaragde veit un alter
1080 U li pilers descent en mer;
Li sacraires fud sardoine,
Li pavemenz calcedoine;
Enz el piler fermét aveit
1084 Tref de fin or: ço susteneit;
E les lampes sunt de beril.
Cil ne crement nul peril;
Ici estunt desque al .iii. jurn;
1088 Messes chantent tuit al lur turn.
Brandans en prent purpens en sei
Ne deit querre le Deu secrei;
Dist as muines: 'Creés mun sen:
1092 Toluns d'ici, alum nus en!'
Un chaliz mult festival
Prent l'abes tut de cristal;
Bien set de Deu ne resortet,
1096 Pur servir l'en quant le portet.

Granz curs unt fait li pelerin,
Mais uncore ne sevent fin.
E nepurtant ne s'en feignent:
1100 Mais cum plus vunt, plus se peinent,
Ne de peiner ne recrerrunt
De ci que lur desir verrunt.
Apparut lur terre truble
1104 De neir calin e de nuble:
De flaistre fum ert fumante,
De caruine plus puante;
De grant nerçun ert enclose.
1108 Cist ne rovent estre en pose,
E de mult luign unt or oït
Que la ne erent guairs goït.
Mult s'esforcent de ailurs tendre,

7b

1075 icel   1083 li p.   1108 am p.   1109 un or

1112   Mais ça estout lur curs prendre
        Quar li venz la les em meinet.
        E li abes bien les enseignet
        E dist lur: 'Bien sachez
1116   Que a enfern estes cachez.
        N'oustes mester unc mais si grant
        Cum or avez de Deu guarant.'
        Brandans ad fait sur eals la cruz.
1120   Bien set, pres est d'enfern li puz:
        Cum plus pres sunt, plus veient mal,
        Plus tenebrus trovent le val.
        Des parfunz vals e des fosses
1124   Lammes ardanz volent grosses.
        De fous sufflanz li venz enruit;
        Nuls tuneirs si halt ne muit.
        Estenceles od les lammes,
1128   Roches ardanz e les flammes
        Par cel air tant halt volent
        Le cler del jurn que lur tolent.

        Cum alouent endreit un munt,
1132   Virent un féd dunt poür unt.
        Forment fud granz icil malfez,
        D'enfern eisit tuz eschalfez;
        Un mail de fer en puin portout:
1136   A un piler asez i out.
        Cum s'aparçout par sun reguard
        As uilz flammanz cum fus chi art,
        E veit iceals, a tart li est
1140   Que sun turment tut i ait prest.
        Jetant flammes de sa gorge
        A granz salz curt en sa forge.
        Revint mult tost od sa lamme
1144   Tute ruge cume flamme.
        Es tenailes dun la teneit   7c
        Fais a dis bofs bien i aveit.
        Halcet le sus vers la nue
1148   E dreit vers eals puis la rue.
        Esturbeiluns plus tost ne vait

1131 Cun

Quant sus en l'air li venz le trait,
Ne li quarel d'arbeleste,
1152 Ne de funde la galeste:
Cum plus halcet e plus enprent,
En alant forces reprent.
Primes depart, puis amasset;
1156 Ne cheot sur eals, ainz passet.
U cheit en mer, iloec art
Cum brüere en un asart,
E mult lunc tens art la lame
1160 En la mer a grant flamme.
Li venz la nef ad cunduite,
Pur quei d'iloec pregnent fuite.
Al vent portant s'en alerent,
1164 Mais la suvent reguarderent:
L'isle virent aluminé
E cuverte de fumé.
Malsfeiz veient millers plusurs;
1168 Criz de dampnez oënt e plurs.
Püur lur vent forment grant
Del fumé chi luign par l'air s'espant.
Endurerent cum melz pourent;
1172 Eschiverent cum plus sourent.
Sainz hoem cum ad plusurs travailz
De faim, de seif, de freiz, de calz,
Ainxe, tristur e granz poürs,
1176 De tant vers Deu creist sis oürs.
Eisi est d'els puis q'unt voüd
U li dampnez sunt reçoüd:
En Deu ferment lur fiance,
1180 N'i aturnent mescreance.
Vunt s'en avant, n'i dutent rien;
Par ço sevent que espleitent bien.
Ne demurat fors al matin
1184 Virent un lu pres lur veisin:
Un munt cuvert de nublece;
Las meineit vent par destrecce.
Vindrent i tost al rivage,
1188 Mais mult ert de halt estage:

1164 reguardernt   1168 dampnez cent e plusurs

Nuis d'els trestuz choisir ne pout
La haltece que li munz out.
Vers la rive plus ne descent
1192 Que la u plus amunt s'estent.
E la terre est tute neire;
Tel nen out en tut lur eire.
Pur quel chose il ne sourent,
1196 Salt en l'uns fors; puis ne l'ourent.
Tuit unt oïd qu'il lur ad dit,
Mais sul l'abes des uilz le vit:
'Seignur, or de vus sui preiez
1200 Pur mes pechez, bien le crëez.'
E li abes le veit traire
A cent malfez chi le funt braire.
Turnent d'iloec, ailurs en vunt;
1204 Reguardent sei quar poür unt.
Del fum li munz est descuverz,
Enfern veient tut aüverz.
Enfers jetet fus e flammes,
1208 Perches ardanz e les lammes,
Peiz e sufre desque as nües,
Puis les receit, quar sunt sües.

Puis les meinct Brandans par mer,
1212 Des signacles les fait armer.
Veient en mer une boche
Si cum ço fust une roche;
E roche fut verablement,
1216 Mais nel quïent crëablement.
Dunc dist l'abes: 'Ne demurum!
Sachum que seit, si i curum.'
Vindrent ila, si truverent
1220 Iço que poi espeirerent:
Sur la roche u sunt venud
Trovent seant homme nud.
Mult ert periz e detirez,
1224 Delacherez e descirez.

1193 est *not in* A   1198 sul abes   1200 meis   1208 perchez
1210 les *not in* A   1214 Ci cum   1215 fust   1216 ne q.
1218 si iccurum

D'un drap liéd sun vis aveit,
A un piler si se teneit.
Fort se teneit a la pere
1228 Que nel rosast le unde arere;
Undes de mer le ferent fort,
Pur quei n'ad fin la süe mort.
Le une le fert, pur poi ne funt;
1232 Le altre detriers jetet l'amunt.
Peril devant, peril desus,
Peril detriers, peril dejus;
Turment grant ad a destre,
1236 Ne l'ad menur a senestre.
Quant l'unde ad fait ses empeintes,
Mult lassement fait ses pleintes:

'**A**! reis, Jesu, de majestét,
1240 Faldrat ma morz n'ivern ne estét?
Jesu, chi moz tut le trone,
Ja est ta mercit itant bone.
Jesu, tant es misericors;
1244 Ert nul' hure que seie fors?
Jesu, li nez de Marie,
Ne sai si jo mercit crie:
Ne puis ne n'os, quar tant forfis
1248 Que jugemenz de mei est pris.'

Quant le oit Brandans issi plaindre,
Unches dolur nen out graindre,
Levet sa main, tuz les seignet,
1252 D'apresmer la mult se peinet.
Cum apresmout, la mer ne mot,
Ne venz ne orrez ne la commot.
Dist lui Brandans: 'Di mei, dolenz,
1256 Pur quai suffres icez turmenz?
De part Jesu, qui tu crïes,
Jo te cumant quel mei dïes;
E certement me di qui es,
1260 E le forfait pur quei ci es.'

8a

1229 mer firent fort 1231 ne fent   1238 les   1240 niverz
1242 J est   1244 sei

Pur le plurer Brandans ne pout
Avant parler, mais dunc se tout.
Cil lui respunt a voiz basse,
1264   Mult ert roie, forment lasse:
'Jo sui Judas qui serveie
Jesu que jo traïseie.
Jo sui qui mun seignur vendi,
1268   E pur le doul si me pendi.
Semblant d'amur fis pur baiser,
Descordai quant dui apaiser.
Jo sui qui sun aveir guardai,
1272   En larecin le debardai;
E le offrande q'um li portout,
Tut' as povres il l'enhortout,
Jo celoue en mes burses:
1276   Puroc me sunt peines surses;
E quidoue que fust celét   *8b*
A lui qui fist cel estelét.
As povres Deu bien defendi;
1280   Or sunt riche, e jo mendi.
Jo sui li fels qui Deu haï,
Le simple agnel as lus trahi.
Quant vi que as mains ert Pilate,
1284   Dunc oi chere forment mate.
Quant vi as mains ert as Judus,
A ceals crüels liverez li pius,
Quant vi que as gabs l'aürouent,
1288   E d'espines coronouent,
Quant vi vilement que fud traitez,
Sachez que fui mult dehaitez.
Puis vi que fud menez tüer;
1292   Le dulz costéd vi sanc süer.
Quant vi qu'en cruz esteit penduz,
E fud a mort de mei venduz,
Les deners tost offri trente;
1296   Cil ne voldrent cuilir rente.
Repentance n'en oi sage,

1265 servie   1266 traie   1267 que   1270 aapaiser   1272 larcin
1273 quin li p.   1282 Li s.   1286 As   1287 lauroueint
1288 de spinis corouneint   1297 Renpentance

Ainz me tuai par ma rage;
E quant confés ne me rendi,
1300 Dampnez sui de di en di.
Tu ne veiz rien de ma peine
Que enz enfern jo demaine;
Cist est repos de mun peril,
1304 Que al samadi prenc al seril.
Dimaine trestut le jurn
Desque al vespere ai tel sujurn,
E del Noël la quinzeine
1308 Ici deport ma grant peine;
E as festes la Marie
Mes granz peines n'i ai dunc mie;
Pasches e a Pentecoste
1312 Fors tant cum veiz n'i ai plus custe;
A feste altre en trestut l'an
N'ai entrebat de mun ahan.
Dïemaine al serir
1316 D'ici m'en voi pur asperir.'
Dunc dist Brandans: 'Or me di,
Itel repos quant as ici,
En quel endreit te demeines
1320 En turmentes e es peines?
E en espeines quel liu as tu?   *8c*
D'ici quant moz, u en vas tu?
Respunt Judas: 'Pres est li lius
1324 A dïables u est li fius.
N'i ad guairs fors sul un poi;
Tant en sui luign que ci nes oi.
Dous enfers ad ci dejuste;
1328 De suffrir les est grant custe.
Mult pres d'ici sunt dui enfern
Que ne cessent estét ne ivern.
Li plus legiers est horribles,
1332 A ceals qu'i sunt mult penibles.
Ço quident cil qui la peinent
Que altre mal vers eals ne meinent.
Fors mei ne set uns suls de nus

1299 confesse   1304 Quel al s.   1308 deportet   1319 deimeines
1321 queliu   1325 po   1330 esteit

1336 Quels des dous seit plus penus;
    N'est nuls plus ait que l'un des dous,
    Mais jo chaitis ai amedous.
    L'uns est en munt e l'altre en val,
1340 E sis depart la mer de sal:
    Les dous enfers mer les depart,
    Mais merveille est que tut ne art.
    Cil del munt est plus penibles,
1344 E cil del val plus horribles:
    Cil pres de l'air calz e sullenz,
    Cil pres de mer freiz e pullenz.
    Ovoec la nuit un jurn sui sus,
1348 Puis altretant demoir en jus.
    A l'un jurn munte, l'altre descent;
    N'est altre fin de mun turment.
    Ne change enfern pur aleger
1352 Mes pur les mals plus agreger.

    Par lundi e nuit e jurn
    En la roe sui en tresturn,
    E jo chaitis, encröez enz,
1356 Turni tant tost cum fait li venz.
    Venz la cunduit par tut cel air:
    Tot dis m'en voi, tot di repair.

    Puis el demain en sui galiz
1360 Cum cil qui est tot acaliz:
    Ultre la mer vol en le val
    A l'altre enfern u tant ad mal.
    Iloces sui tost ferlïez,
1364 De dïables mult escrïez;
    El lit sui mis sur les broches;   *8d*
    Sur mei mettent plums e roches;
    Iloces sui si espëez
1368 Que mun cors tant percét vëez.
    Al mecredi sus sui rüez
    U li perilz m'i est müez:
    Pose del jurn buil en la peiz

1337 de dous   1342 merveil; tuit   1346 del m.   1349 Al lun   1354 ro
1355 encroenz   1359 el d. el sui g.   1362 Al laltre   1371 Puis del

1372 U sui si teinz cum ore veiz;
      Puis sui ostét e mis al rost,
      Entre dous fus liéd al post.
      Li post de fer fichét i est;
1376 Se pur mei nun, pur el n'i est.
      Tant est ruges cume si dis anz
      En fus goüst as fols sufflanz.
      E pur la peiz li fus s'i prent
1380 Pur enforcer le men turment;
      E dunc sui en peiz rüez,
      Pur plus ardeir sui enlüez.
      Ne n'est marbres nuls itant durs
1384 Ne fust remis se fust mis surs,
      Mais jo sui fait a icest' ire
      Que mis cors ne poit defire.
      Itel peine, que que m'anuit,
1388 Ai tut un jurn e une nuit.

      Puis al jusdi sui mis en val,
      E pur suffrir contrarie mal
      Dunc sui mis en un freid leu
1392 Mult tenebrus e forment ceu.
      Tant i ai freid que mei est tart
      Qu'el fu seie qui tant fort art;
      E dunc m'est vis n'est turmente
1396 Que del freid que plus me sente;
      E de chescun si m'est vis
      Ne seit si fort quant enz sui mis.
      Al vendresdi revenc amunt
1400 U tantes morz cuntre mei sunt.
      Dunc m'escorcent trestut le cors
      Que de la pel n'at puint defors.
      En la suie ovoec le sel
1404 Puis me fulent od l'ardant pel;
      Puis revent hastivement
      Tuz nuvels quirs a cel turment.
      Dis feiz le jurn bien m'escorcent,

1372 fui ci   1379 li peiz   1382 lui e.   1384 remis ne fust
1385 f. acce a icest   1386 nuls c.; desire   1389 su   1393 est atart
1402 puig d.

1408   El sel entrer puis me forcent;
       E puis me funt tut cald beivre   *9a*
       Le plum remis od le quivre.
       Al samedi jus me rüent
1412   U li altre mals me müent,
       E puis sui mis en gaiole;
       En tut enfern n'at si fole,
       En tut enfern n'at si orde;
1416   En li descen e sanz corde.
       Iloeces gis, n'i ai lüur,
       En tenebres e en püur.
       Püurs i vent itant grande
1420   Ne guart quant mes quers espande.
       Ne puis vomir pur le quivere
       Que cil la me firent beivre;
       Puis enfle fort, e li quirs tent;
1424   Anguisus sui; pur poi ne fent.
       Tels calz, tels freiz e tels ulurs
       Suffret Judas e tels dolurs.
       Si cum fud er al samedi,
1428   Vinc ci entre nune e midi;
       Hui mei repos a cest sedeir.
       Eneveis avrai mal seir:
       Mil deiables senés vendrunt;
1432   Ne avrai repos quant mei tendrunt.
       Mais si tu es de tel saveir,
       Anuit me fai repos aveir!
       Si tu es de tel merite,
1436   Anuit me fai estre quite!
       Bien sai que tu sainz es e pius,
       Quant sanz reguarz vens a tels lius.'

       Plurout Brandans a larges plurs
1440   D'ico que cist ad tanz dolurs;
       Comandet lui que lui dïet
       Que li dras deit dum se lïet,
       E la pere u il se tint,
1444   Demandet dunt e de qui vint.
       Cil lui respunt: 'En ma vie

1421 vomer   1428 Veinc   1430 Uneveis

Fis poi bien e mult folie.
Li biens e mals or me perent
1448 Quel enz el quer plus chier m'erent.
De l'almoine que jo guardai
A un nud féd drap acatai;
Pur cel ai cest dun me lie
1452 Par la buche, que ne nie.
Quant l'unde vent en le vis devant,
Alques par cest ai de guarant,
Mais en enfern ne me valt rien,
1456 Quant de propre me fud mun bien.
A un' aigue fis un muncel
E puis desus un fort puncel,
U mult home periseient,
1460 Mais puis bien i guariseient:
Puroec ai ci refrigerie
De si grande ma miserie.'

Cum apresmout vers le premseir,
1464 Dunc vit Brandans que cil dist veir:
Vit venir deiables mil
Od turmentes e grant peril;
E venent dreit a cel dolent;
1468 Salt l'uns avant, al croc le prent.
Brandans lur dist: 'Laisez l'ici
Desque al matin que seit lunsdi.'
Cil li dïent e calengent
1472 Ne lairunt pas que nel prengent.
Dunc dist Brandans: 'Jo vus comant,
E de Jesu faz mun guarant.'
Cil le laisent, e a force;
1476 N'i unt nïent a l'estorce.
Brandans estait iloec la nuit;
N'i ad malfez qui mult n'annuit.
Deiables sunt de l'altre part;
1480 Ainz que seit jurz mult lur est tart;
A grant greine, a voiz truble
Dïent que avrat peine duble.
Respunt l'abes: 'Ne avrat turment

9b

1447 pent   1452 neie   1462 manuserie   1463 apremout   1470 lusdi

1484   Plus que ad oüd par jugement.'
E puis qu'il fud cler ajurnét,
Od tut Judas s'en sunt turnét.

Brandans s'en vait d'iloec avant.
1488   Bien set de Deu ad bon guarant;
E li muine bien sevent tuit
Que segur sunt al Deu cunduit;
Mercïent Deu de lur veies
1492   E de tutes lur agreies.
Cum se numbrent li cumpaignun,
En lur cunte failent a l'un,
E ne sevent qu'est devenuz
1496   Ne en quel leu est detenuz.
Des dous sevent cum unt errét,   *9c*
Mais de cest terz sunt enserrét.
L'abes lur dist, qui tut le sout:
1500   'Deus en ad fait ço que li plout.
D'iço n'aiez nule dute,
Ainz tenez bien vostre rute.
Sachez qu'il ad sun jugement
1504   U de repos u de turment.'

Si cum il vunt, veient ester
Un munt mult halt tut sul en mer.
Tost i venent, mais la rive
1508   Roiste lur ert e escive.
L'abes lur dist: 'Istrai m'en fors.
Ne movet uns fors sul nun cors!'
Puiet le munt e lunges vait
1512   Ainz que trovét nule rien ait.
Par un rochét sa veie tint,
Une bodme puis li survint.
Eisit uns hom tost de cel liu,
1516   Religïus semblout e piu.
Cil apelet Brandan avant,
Quar par Deu fud sun nun savant,
Puis le baiset, ses cumpaignuns

1498 terce   1511 Puieit   1512 u nule   1514 p. il s.
1515 Eist   1519 cumpaignus

1520 Dist qu'amenget: ne failet uns.
      Vait i Brandans, fait les venir,
      Funt al rochét le nef tenir.
      Cil ad tuz numez par sei:
1524 'Venez avant e baisez mei!'
      Cil li firent. Puis les menet
      A sun estre, lur enseignet.
      Cil reposent cum lur ad dit.
1528 Merveillent lui e sun habit:
      N'ad vestement fors de sun peil,
      Dum est cuvert si cum de veil;
      Reguard aveit angelïel
1532 E tut le cors celestïel;
      N'est si blance neifs ne clere
      Cumme li peilz d'icest frere.
      Dist lui Brandans: 'Beal pere chers,
1536 Di mei qui es.' Cil: 'Volunters!'
      Jo ai nun Pols li hermites.
      De tuz dolurs sui ci quites.
      Ci ai estét grant e lunc tens,
1540 E ça m'en vinc par Deu asens.
      El secle fui hermite en bois: *9d*
      Cele vie pris en mun cois;
      Secund le sens que aveie poi,
1544 Deu serveie si cume soi.
      Il le cuilit par sa buntét,
      Qu'a plus que n'est le m'at cuntét.
      La me mandat que ci venisse
1548 U ma glorie attendisse.
      Cument i vinc? En nef entrai
      Tute preste cum la truvai;
      Deus me cunduit tost e süef;
1552 Quant arivai, ralat la nef.
      Nunante anz ad qu'ai ci estét.
      Beal tens i ad, tuz dis estét.
      Ici atent le juïse;
1556 De Deu en ai cumandise:
      Trestut i sui en carn e en os

1522 tener   1542 cors   1543 aver   1544 servie   1545 I ble c.
1546 lamat c.

Sanz mal que ai sui en repos;
Dunc a primes al jugement
1560 L'espirit del cors frat seivrement;
Od les justes resuscitrai
Pur la vie que segut ai.
Un sergant oi trent' anz pleiners,
1564 De mei servir suveners:
Uns lutres fud qui m'aportout
Suvent peisun dun il me pout
Tuz dis tres jurs en la semaine;
1568 Unckes nule ne fud vaine
Que treis peisuns ne me portast
Dun aveie pleiner past.
Al col pendud marin werec
1572 Plein un sacel portout tut sec
Dun mes peisuns pouse quire.
Par qui ço fud, bien ert sire!
Es primers anz que vinc ici
1576 Tuz les trent' anz fui poüd si.
Des peisuns fui poüd si bien
N'oi mester de beivre rien;
N'ennuiout puint nostre Seignur
1580 De tel cunreid ne de greignur.
Puis les trent' anz ne revint cil;
Nel fist sur peis ne ne m'out vil,
Mais Deus ne volt que plus de fors
1584 Venist cunreid pur sul mun cors.
Ici me fist la funtaine   *10a*
De tuz cunreiz qui est pleine:
Ço li est vis qui rien en beit
1588 De tuz cunreiz que saüls seit.
De aigue ai vescut anz seisante,
Trent' a peisun: sunt nonante.
En le mund fui anz cinquante:
1592 Mis ethez est cent e quarante.
Frere Brandan, or te ai dit
Cument ici ai mun delit.
Mais tu iras en paraïs;

1558 que ai] quar   1563 Uns s.   1571 A c.   1586 cunreid
1588 cunreid

1596 Pres ad set anz que tu l'as quis.
　　　Arere fras anceis return
　　　Al bon hoste u ous sujurn:
　　　Il te menrat e tu le siu
1600 En paraïs u sunt li piu.
　　　D'icest' aigue porte en od tei,
　　　Dum guarisses de faim e sei.
　　　Entre en ta nef; ne demurer!
1604 Ne deit sun vent hom sururer.'
　　　Dunet cungét e cil le prent;
　　　De ses bienfaiz graces l'en rent.

　　　Or turnent vers lur hoste,
1608 Si unt niule mult enposte.
　　　Siglent lunges ainz que veingent,
　　　Ja seit ço que dreit curs teingent,
　　　E al jusdi de la ceine
1612 La i venent a grant peine.
　　　Iloec estunt, cum soleient,
　　　Desque la que muveir deient.
　　　Le samadi al peisun vunt:
1616 Cum altres anz la feste i funt,
　　　E bien sevent qu'or ad set anz
　　　Que li peisuns est lur servanz.
　　　Deu en loient: n'i unt perte
1620 Pur la vertud de Deu certe.
　　　E l'endemain d'iloec movent
　　　A itel vent cum il trovent.
　　　Vers les oiseals tut dreit en vunt
1624 La u dous meis sujurnerunt.
　　　Iloec estunt a grant deduit,
　　　E atendent le bon cunduit
　　　Del bon hoste qui frat od eals
1628 L'eire qui est tant bons e beals.
　　　Cil aprestet tuz lur busuinz　　　　　　　　　*10b*
　　　Quar bien saveit que l'eire est luinz;
　　　E bien set tut que lur estot,
1632 Pur ço guarnist de quanque poet.
　　　Entrent en mer, l'ostes ovoec;

1598 u uus s.　　　1601 portez od　　　1604 sun nen　　　1614 muver　　　1616 ainz

Ne revendrunt jamais iloec.
Tendent lur curs vers orïent.
1636 De l'esguarer n'i funt nïent:
Tel i at enz en qui cunduit
Vunt a goie e a deduit.
A curs entrin sanz defalte
1640 Quarante dis en mer halte
Eisi curent que ne lur pert
Fors mer e cel qui sur eals ert.
E par l'otreid del rei divin
1644 Or aprisment vers le calin
Qui tut aclot le paraïs
Dunt Adam fud poëstis.
Nües grandes tenerge funt,
1648 Que li sun eir return n'i unt:
Li granz calins tant aorbet,
Qui i entret, tuz asorbet,
Si de Deu n'at la veüe
1652 Qui poust passer cele nue.
Dunc dist l'ostes: 'Ne i targez,
Mais la sigle de vent chargez!'
Cum aprisment, part la nue
1656 A l'espace d'une rue.
Cil se metent enz el calin
E parmi unt grant chemin.
Mult se fïent en lur hoste
1660 Pur la nue q'unt en coste:
Grant est forment e serree,
De ambes parz est amassee.
Treis jurz curent tut a dreit curs
1664 Par le chemin que lur est surs.
El quart issent de cel calin;
Forment sunt léd li pelerin.
De la nue eisut s'en sunt
1668 E paraïs bien choisit unt.
Tut en primers uns murs lur pert
Desque as nües qui halcez ert:
N'i out chernel ne aleür

1639 c. enclin   1648 le s. e.   1653 l'ostes *not in A*   1660 que qunt

1672 Ne bretache ne nule tur.
Nuls d'els ne set en feid veire 10c
Quel il seit faiz de materie,
Mais blancs esteit sur tutes neifs:
1676 Faitres fud li suverains reis.
Tuz ert entrins, sanz antaile,
Unc al faire n'out travaile,
Mais les gemmes funt granz lüurs
1680 Dum purplantez esteit li murs.
As gutes d'or grisolites
Mult i aveit d'isselites;
Li murs flammet, tut abrase,
1684 De topaze, grisopase,
De jargunce, calcedoine,
D'esmaragde e sardoine;
Jaspes od les amestistes
1688 Forment luisent par les listes;
Li jacinctes clers i est il
Od le cristal e od le beril;
L'un a l'altre dunet clartét:
1692 Chis asist fud mult enartét.
Lüur grande s'entreportent
Des colurs chi si resortent.
Li munt sunt halt, de marbre dur,
1696 U la mer bat mult luign del mur;
E desur le munt marbrin
La muntaine est tute d'or fin;
E puis desus esteit li murs
1700 De paraïs qui clot les flurs.
Tels est li murs, si surplantez,
Qui doust estre de nus hantez.
Tendent tut dreit vers la porte,
1704 Mais l'entree mult ert forte:
Draguns i at qui la guardent;
Si cume fus trestut ardent.
Dreit a l'entrer pent uns glavies,
1708 Qui cel ne creint nen est savies,

1672 brestache   1674 maiterie   1675 nefs   1676 Fatters
1679 grant   1690 biril   1696 mult *expuncted before* luign   1698 Li m.
1704 entre; fort   1708 creit

La mure aval, le helte amunt;
Ne me merveille si poür unt.
En aines pent, e turnïet;
1712 Sul del vedeir esturdïet.
Fer ne roche ne adamant
Ne pot guarir a sun trenchant.
Puis unt veüd un juvencel
1716 Qui veint cuntre eals, forment bel;
E cil se fait Deu message,   *10d*
Dist que vengent a rivage.
Il arivent; cil les receit,
1720 Tuz les numet par lur nun dreit;
Puis dulcement les ad baisez,
E les draguns tuz apaisez:
Fait les gesir cuntre terre
1724 Mult humlement e sanz guerre;
E le glaive fait retenir
A un angele qu'il fait venir;
E l'entree est uverte:
1728 Tuit entrent en glorie certe.

Avant en vait cil juvenceals,
Par paraïs vait ovoec eals.
De beals bois e de rivere
1732 Veient terre mult plenere.
Gardins est la praierie
Qui tuz dis est beal flurie.
Li flur süef mult i flairent,
1736 Cum la u li piu repairent,
D'arbres, de flurs delicïus,
De fruit, d'udurs mult precïus;
De runceie ne de cardunt
1740 Ne de orthie n'i ad fusun;
D'arbre n'erbe n'i ad mie
Ki süaté ne rechrie.
Flurs e arbres tuz dis chargent,
1744 Ne pur saisun unc ne targent;
Estét süef tuz dis i est,

1709 Lamur *or* Lai nur   1711 e *not in A*   1716 veient   1724 gurre
1729 Quant   1733 Grandins   1745 Esteit

Li fruiz de arbres e de flurs prest,
Bois repleniz de veneisun,
1748 E tut li flum de bon peisun.
Li flum i sunt qui curent lait.
Cele plentét par tut en vait:
La ruseie süet le mel
1752 Par le ruseit qui vient del cel.
Si munt i at, cil est de or;
Si grande pere n'a en tensor.
Sanz fin i luist li clers soleil,
1756 Ne venz n'orez n'i mot un peil,
N'i vient nule nue de l'air
Qui del soleil tolget le clair.
Chi ci estrat, mal n'i avrat,
1760 Ne de mals venz ja ne savrat,
Ne chalz ne freiz ne dehaite   *11a*
Ne faim ne seit ne suffraite.
De tuz ses bons avrat plentét.
1764 Ço que plus est sa voluntét,
Cel ne perdrat, süurs en est;
Tuz dis l'avrat e truvrat prest.
Bien veit Brandans cele goie.
1768 L'ure li semblet forment poie
Qu'il i estait a ço vedeir;
Lunges voldrat iloec sedeir.
Mult bien avant l'ad cil menét,
1772 De multes riens l'ad asenét:
Bien diviset e si li dit
De quel avrat chascuns delit.
Vait cil avant e cist aprés
1776 Sur un halt munt cume ciprés;
D'ici veient avisïuns
Dum ne sevent divisïuns.
Angeles veient e sis oient
1780 Pur lur venir cum s'esgoient.
Oient lur grant melodie,
Mais nel poient suffrir mie:

1749 Li f. isurent ci c.   1753 Ci   1754 pere a tensor
1760 nel   1767 vait   1768 Lur le s.
1773 divisit

Lur nature ne poet prendre
1784 Si grant glorie, ne entendre.
Cil lur ad dist: 'Returnum nus!
Avant d'ici ne menrai vus;
Ne vus leist pas aler avant,
1788 Quar poi estes a ço savant.
Brandans, tu veis cest paraïs
Que tu a Deu mult requeïs.
De la glorie cent mil tant
1792 Que n'as veüd, ad ça avant.
A ore plus n'i aprendras,
Devant içoe que revendras.
O or venis ci carnalment
1796 Tost revendras spiritalment.
Or t'en reva; ci revendras,
Le juïse ci atendras.
De cez peres en fai porter
1800 A enseignes de conforter.'
Puis que out ço dist, il en alat,
Enseignes de paraïs portat.
Brandans de Deu cungét ad pris
1804 E as chers sainz de paraïs.
Li juvenceals les en cunduit: *11b*
Desqu'en la nef sunt entrét tuit,
Puis ad sur eals seignacle fait.
1808 Mult tost unt sus lur sigle trait.
Iloec remist lur hostes pius,
Quar paraïs fud sis dreiz fius.
E cil s'en vunt haitément;
1812 Nen unt d'orez retenement:
En treis meis sunt en Irlande
Par la vertud de Deu grande.
La nuvele vait par païs
1816 Que venuz est de paraïs.
Ne sunt haitét sul li parent,
Ainz sunt trestuz comunement.
Sur tuz sunt liéd li cher frere
1820 De ço qu'or unt lur dulz pere.
Suvent lur dist cum unt errét,

1787 list   1790 as D.   1815 Ja   1819 chere f.

U furent bien u enserrét;
E si lur dist cum prest truvat
1824   Quanque busuign a Deu ruvat,
E l'un e l'el trestut lur dist,
Cum il truvat ço que il quist.
Li plusurs d'els ensaintirent
1828   Par la vertud qu'en lui virent.
Tant cum Brandans el secle fud,
A mulz valut par Deu vertud.
Quant vint al tens que il finat,
1832   Ralat u Deus lui destinat.
El regne Deu, u alat il,
Par lui en vunt plusur que mil.

1822 *second* u *not in* A
1834 *after this line follows*: Explicit vita sancti brandani

Notes to the text

These notes are intended to facilitate the understanding of the text not only by elucidating grammatical difficulties and offering translations of particular passages, but also by providing a certain amount of background literary material to supplement that given in the Introduction. Notes followed by the mention '(W.)' indicate our indebtedness to the corresponding notes of Waters's edition. For the use of abbreviated titles, see p. 27 above.

1–18. The subject of the first sentence of this prologue is postponed until l. 8: 'My lady Queen Adeliza, through whom the law of God will prevail and the law of men grow stronger, and through whom an end will be put to all this warring by virtue of King Henry's might and by the counsel that you will provide, the envoy Dom Benedeit greets you a thousand times and a thousand more. To the best of his ability he has embarked upon the task that you set and undertaken to put down in writing (Latin? and) in French, as you told him, the story of the good abbot, St Brendan. But protect him from being mocked, since he tells what he knows and does what he can: it is not right to reproach such a servant. But someone who is capable and yet is not willing, should properly be made to suffer.'

1. For *Aaliz*, see Intro., pp. 4–5.

8. For *Benedeiz*, see Intro., pp. 5–6.

10. W. emends *entremis* to *en letre mis* on the basis of other manuscripts, even though this involves direct repetition with the next line. Our simple addition of *e* avoids this and gives a satisfactory sense (on this use of *entremetre*, see TL 3, 666; Gdf. 3, 291c).

11. W. translates *letre* as 'writing', but Professor Legge, *MLR* 56 (1961), 333–4, has shown that the meaning 'Latin' is equally possible. At all events, if Benedeit did in fact write a Latin version, it has not survived.

13. For an account of the historical Brendan, see Introduction, pp. 1–2. The spelling of the saint's name with *e* in the first syllable is the older form and is found in Latin texts in Low German areas; see C. Selmer, *Scriptorium* 10 (1956), 256–9. For rhymes with the name *Brendan*, see Intro., p. 13.

16. We have disregarded the scribe's word-division with the group *es-*, as in *n'esteot* for *ne steot*, in the interests of easier comprehensibility.

19 ff. In conformity with Old Irish custom, Brendan's ancestry is given, albeit briefly. Unlike most Irish tales, this text makes no mention of specific relatives or place of birth which would presumably be of little interest to an Anglo-Norman audience. (The *NB* has such details; see Selmer, pp. 3, 83, and

J. Carney, *Medium Aevum* 32 (1963), 37–44.) It was also customary in Latin and French saints' lives to indicate whatever was noteworthy about a saint's birth or heritage, in this case his 'royal' lineage. There is, incidentally, no foundation for crediting Brendan with royal blood.

24–6. This is not an exact biblical quotation but renders the sense of, for example, Matthew 6: 19–21 and Luke 9: 24–5 (W.).

27–32. W. punctuates this passage differently, taking *dras de moine* 29 as an apposition to *veirs* 28 and placing a stop after *eisil* 30; cf. A. Långfors's review of W.'s edition, *Romania* 55 (1929), 568–71.

33. *Par art de lui* 'through his skill, ability'. The construction is not unknown in early texts; cf. *Roland* 1268, 1553.

39–43. The construction here is paratactical; l. 39 looks forward to l. 43: . . . *prist en purpens [que] ne fereit fin de prïer Deu.*

41. The rhyme *rustes* (= *ruistes*) : *justes* is imperfect and isolated. There is one instance (1573) of the reduction of the diphthong [yi] or [ui], but it is to [i] and not [y] or [u]; see Intro., p. 13.

47 ff. The Anglo-Norman author attributes Brendan's desire to see the Other World to his own faith and curiosity, whereas in *NB* the desire springs from hearing Barintus's account of his own journey given when he comes to visit Brendan; cf. ll. 73ff.

48. *prïer prent* The more frequent construction is *prendre a* + infinitive with the sense 'begin to'; cf. 284, 501, 596. Another example without *a* is *pregnent oser* 307; cf. also *prent avaler* 868.

53–4. Anglo-Norman regularly retains apparently unmetathesised forms of semi-learned words such as GLORIA, HISTORIA, VICTORIA etc. which survive through to Mod. Eng. in *glory*, *history*, *victory* etc. (Pope § 1105). The -*orie* suffix, however, counts for two, and not three, syllables here and elsewhere in our text (cf. 541, 1027), which suggests that the pronunciation was similar to the Continental French equivalent *gloire*, *estoire*, *victoire* etc. (cf. also *refrigerie* : *miserie* 1461, *veire* : *materie* 1673 and the note to l. 1707); cf. also W. p. cxliii, § xx.

55. *voldret*, if not a variant spelling for a conditional *voldreit*, is to be seen as a relic of the Latin pluperfect indicative but with a preterite meaning (cf. Moignet, 77, 259).

59–60. 'He prays God unceasingly [that] he show him that [place] clearly'; an example of parataxis which is a characteristic feature of Benedeit's syntax; cf. Intro., p. 15, ll. 121–2, 205–6, 384, 1285–6 etc.

75. The historical Barintus (d. 548 or 552) was a kinsman and confidant of St Brendan and himself a cleric, becoming Abbot of Drumscullen. He is mentioned in only one other literary work besides the *Brendan*, the *Vita Merlini* of Geoffrey of Monmouth, in which he pilots King Arthur to the Fortunate Isles (see ed. J. J. Parry, ll. 929–31). Nowhere is he mentioned as making a voyage to the Promised Land, nor even as being a monk. It has been argued that the figure of Barintus was originally a seagod who in earlier Celtic literature and in *NB* had been changed into a saint; cf. Selmer, p. 99.

85. *Mernoc* is a hypocoristic or pet name derived from that of one of his ancestors, Ernan of Inis Caín (Fair Island) and is preserved in the Scottish place-name Kilmarnock. The 'Fair Island', not named in our text, appears in

NB as the site of Barintus's monastery and called the *Insula Deliciosa*, identified by C. Plummer as an island in Donegal Bay; see J. Carney, *op. cit.*, p. 39.

86. *cist* = Barintus.

90. This is the reading proposed by W.

94. W. relates *cisle* to OP *cislar* which is itself derived from Latin FISTULARE
'to play a pipe, flute, etc.', though the word has clearly undergone some
onomatopoeic confusion with *sifler* < SIBILARE.

97–8. 'for that island to which Saint Mernoc had sailed was so near [to
Paradise that] he led a life of Paradise [there] and could hear the angels'.

108. *Tuz* is adverbial rather than adjectival here: 'the very best'.

115. *En* is to be taken with *meint*; *ques* = *que les*: 'They begged him to take
them along with him'.

117–20. 'The reason I tell you this is that I wish to be sure of you before I
take you away from here, rather than have to regret it afterwards', or alternatively: '. . . rather than take you away and later regret it'.

121–2. 'They give assurance [that] there will be no delay on their account'.

127–8. 'We have no idea how difficult what we have envisaged is'.

133–4. 'And let us fast for three days in every week for a period of forty
days'.

140. Cf. note to l. 356.

157. Our text has several examples of scribal *le* for *la*; cf. *le arbre blanche*
849, and ll. 652, 928, 950, 1147, 1522.

158. 'To the place where he knew, from God, that he was to embark'.

164. Corresponding to *le Salt Brandan NB* has (§ 4) *sedes Brendani* 'Brendan's Seat' (identified with present-day Brandon Head on the Dingle Penin-
sula), though earlier in § 2 it had spoken of *Saltus virtutum Brendani* to
describe the site of Brendan's abbey at Clonfert. Benedeit would appear to
have transferred the Latin *saltus* 'meadow' from the earlier context to here,
and to have linked it to OF *salt* meaning 'leap'. The obvious parallel which
springs to mind is Tristan's Leap, a rock on to which, as Beroul explains (ll. 948
ff), Tristan dramatically jumped from a chapel to avoid capture. Beroul's
wording 'Encor claiment Cornualan / Cele pierre le Saut Tristran' (953–4)
might even seem to echo Benedeit's 'que li vilain / Or apelent le Salt Brandan'.
Cf. for this and other possible connections between the *Brendan* and OF
romances, M. D. Legge, 'Anglo-Norman Historiography and the Romances'
in *Medievalia et Humanistica* n.s. 6 (1975), 41–9. On Tristan's and other
similar leaps, cf. A. Ewert's ed. of Beroul, vol. II (Oxford, 1970), pp. 138–9.

173–80. There is less detail on the construction of the currach here than in
NB, which explains (§ 4) that the ribs and frame were made of timber (wicker
in some Mss.), as was the custom in those parts, that the covering was tanned
oxhides *rubricatis in roborina cortice*, which would appear to mean that the
hides had been seasoned between strips of oak bark. The seams of the boat
were caulked *ex butiro* by which is meant wool grease or animal fat (the more
usual pitch would have been 'bitumine'), and a mast, sail and rudder were
fitted. Cf. T. Severin, *op. cit.*, ch. 2 and appendix III.

175. We assume that *avolst*, which clearly means 'covered' at 176, is also
implicit in this line with the meaning of 'lined'.

177. Not only does Ms. *juindre* 'join' seem less appropriate than *uindre* 'caulk' in the context, but as W. points out, *juindre* would conflict with the text of *NB*.

185. W.'s word-division *enenz* (also 280) has been adopted by TL 3, 308, but these are the only examples listed.

193. *A tei entrer*, which seems to have the sense of 'accompany you, enter your service', might show the analogical influence of *estre a* 'be a vassal of'. TL 3, 676–9 registers nothing similar.

200. Abiram and Dathan revolted against the authority of Moses, and the earth opened and swallowed them up: Numbers 16: 1–33.

224. *Que* is no doubt for *qui = cui* 'whose', though it could also be construed as a conj. W. suggests that *cesset*, which makes an imperfect rhyme with *amonestet*, was originally *cestet* 'stumbles', and corrects accordingly.

228. *Idunc* 'then, in these circumstances', according to Moignet p. 290, "marque une certaine vivacité de ton".

232. *Aler = haler* 'haul'.

236. It is difficult to see what meaning can be attributed to *par nul desdeign*. (For negative *nul*, see note to l. 630).

239. 'They lose strength as their food runs out'. This construction seems to combine the two figures of rhetoric zeugma and hysteron-proteron.

252. *Eschiper* in OF normally means 'embark', though the context here (confirmed by *NB*, *L* and *M*) demands the sense, unattested elsewhere, of 'moor, make fast' (W.).

267. In *NB* they are led to this place by a dog; Selmer, pp. 13–14.

275–6. For the rhyme *clarté : entailét*, see Intro., p. 13.

287–93. The *Voyage of Mael Duin* also mentions an island where food, drink and shelter are ready for travellers; ch. 6, p. 469.

305. For this construction see M. Pelan, 'Old French *s'oublier* . . .' in *Romanistisches Jahrbuch* 10 (1959), 59–77.

307. 'They venture (*lit*. begin to dare? cf. 48) to spend the night' (W.).

310. In *NB*, p. 75, Brendan sees the devil in the form of a black baby, a not infrequent image according to Selmer, p. 85 n. 26.

315. *hanap* 'communion cup, chalice'. *NB* has a *frenum argenteum* in this episode which, Selmer suggests, p. 85, n. 27, could be translated as 'necklace' rather than the conventional 'bridle'. In the *Voyage of Mael Duin* one of the three latecomers, Maelduin's fosterbrothers, also steals a necklace for which crime he is struck down and turned to ashes by a fiery cat. A similar incident occurs in the *Perlesvaus*, ll. 125–77 (eds. W. A. Nitze and T. A. Jenkins), where a squire, Cahus, steals a candelabra from a chapel and subsequently dies for the theft. Marjorie Williamson compares all three episodes in *Modern Philology* 30 (1932), 5–11.

335–7. 'He (the thief) realised that the abbot knew of the theft, [and understood] how he had come to know of it'. This is, perhaps, the boldest example of *enjambement* in the text, and the sense is not altogether clear. Cf. W.'s note.

336. *larecin*, correctly spelt at 319, here appears in the Ms. as *larcein* with the *r* added in superscript. At 1272 it appears as *larcin* with *i* added interlinearly over an expuncted *e*. Given this scribal confusion, we have emended the two variant spellings to conform with that of 319.

356. This is the first appearance of the messenger, announced in l. 140, who appears at various times throughout the story, providing the travellers with food, and helping them find their way to Paradise. Also referred to as *lur hoste* (825 etc., as well as *mes* 405 and *le Deu fedeil* 580), this guardian angel remains in Paradise when Brendan and his companions return to Ireland (1809–10).

382. 'As far away as they could see (*lit.* . . . as it could be clear to them)'.

386. This is *ariver* in its etymological sense (< *ADRIPARE) of 'come to shore, land'.

390. *Ces landes* shows the so-called 'epic' or descriptive use of the demonstrative replacing the definite article and connoting generalised familiarity: 'il sert à présenter la notion du substantif comme bien connue, notoire, quasi constante dans le genre de situation évoqué' (Moignet, 113).

393. *La ceine* is specifically the Last Supper, more generally Holy Communion. Here the reference is to Maundy Thursday, called *jusdi absolud* at 822. Cf. note to ll. 829–30.

397. *Dunt* 'that with which'.

402. 'Since we now find no one else here [from whom to ask leave]'.

410. *Grant* for *granz* before a pl. obj. is encountered also at 609.

414. 'I do not know if he was forthcoming (?), but he told him little about it'. Cf. the use of *oser* at 307 above.

415–16. 'We have all that our hearts could desire (*lit.* . . . that we can think of in our hearts)'.

425. *Entras* looks like a syncopated future form of *entreras*. The other Mss. have *estras*.

439. *Qui* 'he whom'; cf. *que* 923.

442 ff. The fact that Brendan stays aboard shows his foreknowledge of events, and when the whale begins to move, he is ready to explain what has happened to his startled companions and to draw an appropriate moral. The meal on the whale's back is perhaps the best known episode of the *Brendan* legend, and was a favorite subject in medieval iconography, finding its way particularly into illustrated bestiaries; cf. F. McCulloch, *Medieval Latin and French Bestiaries* (Chapel Hill, N.C., 1960), esp. pp. 91–2.

462. For examples of the OF phrase *parmi tot ço* 'even so', apparently unknown to W. (cf. his gloss 'during' s.v. *parmi*), see TL 7, 310–11; cf. also *Horn* II, p. 107, and A. Bell in *Romania* 97 (1976), 475–7.

471. *Sur* 'more than' i.e. 'Bigger than'; cf. 702.

477–8. This is a clear reference to Genesis 1: 21 where whales are the first creatures created: 'And God created whales, and every living creature that moveth. . . .'

481 ff. The Island of Birds. Similar episodes occur in *Mael Duin* pp. 493–5, *Hui Corra*, p. 49, and *Snegdus and Mac Riagla*, p. 21, and find echoes in medieval vision literature where souls are depicted in bird form (see below 519), as well as in Arthurian literature, notably Chrétien de Troyes's *Yvain* where the beautiful tree guarding Esclados le Roux's storm-creating fountain becomes the roost for a multitude of harmonious birds when the storm ends (ed. M. Roques, ll. 380–5, 413–18, 459–75); see also S. Méjean, 'A propos de l'arbre aux oiseaux dans *Yvain*', *Romania* 91 (1970), 392–9 for possible Arabic influences. M. Donatus, *Beasts and Birds in the Lives of Early Irish Saints* (Philadelphia, 1934), pp. 242–3, reminds us that Giraldus Cambrensis in his description of Ireland (ed. Dimock, ll. 5124 ff) refers to ' "sanctuaries", not primarily for men alone, but for birds and beasts in honour of the patron saints Saint Beanus and Saint Brendan', and sees in this concern for animals and birds early motivation for stories later associated with St Francis (p. 244). Cf. Selmer, p. 86 n. 31.

484. 'they are not afraid (*lit*. do not avoid) to land'.

489. *Arbre* with feminine gender is attested more readily at 849. Similarly masc. *isle* is apparently found at 93, 97, 423 etc. (cf. also note to 1165). Since both of these genders recur in Anglo-Norman (see *The Anglo-Norman Alexander*, vol. II (ANTS 32–3, London, 1977), p. 47), this is probably a dialectal feature. A parallel to masc. *flur* 96 occurs in Chardri's *Josaphaz* (ed. J. Koch, 1. 1964; cf. also *Roland* 2871–2), and to masc. *dulur* 1440, 1538 in Philippe de Thaün's *Bestiaire* (ed. E. Walberg, 1. 2830). *Sigle*, usually masc. in our text, is found once as a fem. (1654); *mer* is also perhaps encountered once with a masc. adj. (see note to 1. 883).

491–2. No description as precise is given in *NB* and one wonders whether Benedeit was aware of the corresponding episode in *Snegdus and Mac Riagla* (p. 21) where the birds perched in the tree 'used to beat their sides with their wings, so that showers of blood dropt out of their sides for dread of the signs of Doom'.

493. 'as high as the eye could see'. W. glosses *par vedue* 'judging by the eye'.

504. 'what is the meaning of such a great abundance of birds'; cf. *que tu deies* 516 'what your purpose is'.

510. 'like the sound (*lit*. striking) of a bell'.

519 ff. Fallen angels who were spared the torments of Hell for refusing to join Satan, yet denied their abode in Heaven because they were unfaithful to God, occur elsewhere in medieval literature, notably in Dante's *Inferno* III, 37–42 ('quel cattivo coro / Degli angeli che non furon ribelli / Né fur fedeli a Dio'). For a review of the literary occurrences of these 'neutral' angels, see M. Dando, *Cahiers d'Etudes Cathares*, 2e série, 69 (1976), 1–28. Dando neglects to mention that angels appear in the *Brendan* texts in the form of birds and notes no other such example. Souls in the form of birds were not uncommon in Irish literature; see Selmer, p. 87 n. 32.

536. *Tant* 'this much' anticipates 537–8; *itant* 539 has the same meaning.

545–8. The notion of a seven-year voyage belongs to the *NB* tradition. In *VB* there are two voyages, the first lasting five years and ending unsuccessfully because, according to St Íde Brendan's fostermother, his currach was made of the skins of once living creatures; the second voyage which lasts a further two years, hence the seven, is made in a boat of timber which reaches the Blessed Isle that Brendan had earlier seen in a vision.

550. Noting a similar use of *amunt aval* in Thomas's *Tristan* 2993, L. Foulet, *Romania* 69 (1946–7), 38–9, says: 'Il est clair qu'ici *amont* et *aval* n'indiquent ni une montée ni une descente, mais un mouvement à la surface de la mer qui entraîne le navire tantôt dans un sens tantôt dans le sens opposé. . . .' Here the sense is indeed something like 'back and forth', perhaps even 'all over'.

554. *devalat* The preterite, as is common in OF, serves the function of the pluperfect.

569. *cumplie* 'compline', the last of the canonical hours, hence the last service of the day; cf. *matines* 576, the first service of the day. See also the note to l. 1428 below.

593. *eissil* = *eissi le*.

599. *A remüers* 'to change, as replacements'; cf. *Horn* 2488 *aveir a remüer* 'have a change (of clothes)', and TL 8, 765.

602. '[so that] they do not perish for lack [of provisions]'.

616. This transitive use of *entrer*, surviving into Mod. Eng., seems to be characteristic of Anglo-Norman (there are four examples in *Horn*; cf. also TL 3, 679).

617. *Albeu* is a determinant of *l'isle;* cf. *l'isle Albeu* 784, 876. Saint Ailbe, one of the earliest of Irish saints (d. *c*. 530), was Bishop of Emly (County Tipperary) and patron saint of Munster. According to legend, he had been suckled by a she-wolf, and later, like Brendan, set out in search of the Promised Land. An episode of the *Hui Corra* (ch. 68–9) tells of an island whose inhabitants had arrived there after St Ailbe and followed his rule.

620. *Tut* may be for *tost* 'straight away' (as in the other Mss., though cf. the next line), but could conceivably be read with *al vent* as a reinforcing adv. (cf. *lur nef est tut en brande* 900).

630. Usually in OF the adj. *nul* has positive value (cf. two lines below where *nul* = 'any') unless used in conjunction with the verbal negation *ne*. Here, however, *nepuroec* 629 can hardly fulfil this function. There is another example of negative *nul* without *ne* at 786 (cf. also earlier 236). Although it might be tempting to regard this as an Anglo-Normanism (cf. A. R. Harden's comment in *La Vie de Seint Auban*, p. xxviii), Continental examples are also found, notably in Chrétien's *Erec* (2972) and *Yvain* (3468). Cf. W.'s note to l. 788.

652. 'They keep their very great thirst in check'. *Seif* can be both masc. and fem. in OF, though in our text *le* is sometimes found for *la* (cf. note to 1.157). Cf. Mss. *B* and *D*: *E lur grant sei mult la prement*.

655–6. 'They would have been afraid had it not been for the [monk's] habit [which he was wearing]'.

663. The scribe's spelling seems to confuse etymological *seign* with the semi-learned form *signe* required by the rhyme with *digne*.

668. On scribal *duce* for *dulz*, cf. *dulce* for *dulz* 699 and *terce* for *tierz* 1498; see also Intro., p. 12.

669. *Aler* with the auxiliary *aveir* has the sense of 'journey, walk' in OF (Moignet, 183).

680. *Encassét* for fem. pl. *encassees* sacrifices grammar for rhyme.

686. W. is no doubt right to emend *clers* to *cleres* since this not only gives the extra syllable needed, but also brings the gender of *haspes* into line with the fem. gender of Old English *hæpse* from which it derives. This English word, as well as *raps* 461 'ropes', also at the rhyme, can be used as evidence of insular influence on Benedeit's French.

707. The Miserere is one of the Penitential Psalms (Psalm LI: 'Have mercy upon me, O God . . .').

710. The verbal prefix *re-*, as it does often in OF, has the sense 'for their part'.

719–20. 'It is eighty years since the pilgrim St Ailbe died (*lit.* took his end)'.

W.'s assumption (p. 203) that *prist* has an (unexpressed) impersonal subject allows him to retain *a* of 720, thus preserving correct syllable count, but it obliges him at the same time to correct Ms. *li pelerin* (which we take to be subj.) to *le pelerin*. Cf. *prist decés* 736 with Ailbe as subj.

721 ff. These lines describing Ailbe's life are not derived from *NB*; cf. note to l. 617.

743. *loreür* 'workman, servant' < *LAURATOREM; cf. more usual OF *laborëor*.

749–50. *men : son* These could not rhyme as they stand and W. supposes an original rhyme *mien : suen*, which though infrequent is paralleled elsewhere, e.g. Beroul 3583.

755. 'at the appropriate times (*lit.* at the hours that we ought) . . .'.

758. 'is not used up any the more'. The use of *le* is perhaps an Anglo-Normanism; cf. *Seint Auban*, p. xxvii.

760. 'we have no brother [whose task it is] to look after [the lamps]'. Cf. the use of the indicative in the same construction at ll. 135 and 286.

765. *dublat* 'increased, augmented' not 'doubled'; cf. *meitez* 950 'portions' not 'halves' (W.).

767. 'a week after Epiphany'; cf. 586, 778.

777–8. Brendan has arrived at the Isle of Ailbe for Christmas (cf. l. 618) and is to depart eight days after Epiphany, 13 Jan. (W.). *La semaine* is an apposition to the following line.

779. The oblique form *le jurn*, which is the subject of *vint*, may well have been determined by its function as antecedent of objective *que*.

789 ff. On the Coagulated Sea, which follows the Intoxicating Spring episode in *NB*, see Selmer, p. 88, n. 55. This incident recurs frequently in later medieval literature, particularly in Middle High German.

797. W. corrects *tel* to *tele* for correct syllable count, as he does also at 1194, but this particular analogical form is nowhere attested in our text.

799 ff. The Intoxicating Spring. This incident occurs in similar stories in various forms: as water as sweet as milk in *Snegdus and Mac Riagla*, as the devil's well in *Mael Duin*, as a river of wine in *Hui Corra* and as *aqua suavissima* in the Latin life of Saint Malo; cf. Selmer, p. 88 n. 54.

800. W., following Ms. *B*, corrects to *a plus que cenz* 'by more than hundreds'.

801–2. These two lines are obscure and puzzled the copyists of all the manuscripts. We emend following W. who translates: 'They have need of herbs which are in the boggy ground around the river-bed'. Alternatively: 'the herbs . . . are useful to them'; cf. TL 5, 1709.

812. 'some for a day, some for two . . .'.

829–30. *mandét* 'ritual washing of feet performed on Maundy Thursday'. The action recalls Christ's washing of the feet of his disciples on the day before his crucifixion (John 13: 14). The word itself is derived from Latin *mandatum novum*, the new commandment given by Christ in John 13: 34: 'A new commandment I give you, that ye love one another, as I have loved you, that ye also love one another'. The verse is sung in the liturgy for Maundy Thursday. *Maundy* entered the English language from AN *maundé*.

837. The name *jacoines* representing *Jasconius* of *NB* has been preserved only by our Ms. It is derived from Irish *iasc* 'fish'; see Selmer, pp. 100–1.

844. W. corrects *hure* to *hures* 'services at canonical hours', but sing. *hure* most likely refers to the appointed hour of their departure.

865. The rhyme is between [ẽjn] and [ãjn] (cf. Intro., p. 13), *chaines* being a spelling variant of OF *chaeines*.

866. *Set* was no doubt originally *uit*, or more likely *.viii.*; cf. the reading of Mss. *D*, *E* and *F*. To the seven weeks separating Easter and Pentecost is to be added the octave of Pentecost of l. 862.

868. '. . . comes swooping down'.

883. Despite W.'s contention that *parfunt* here is an adverb, it is not easy to translate it otherwise than as an adj., albeit masc. in form qualifying *mer*.

890. W. corrects Ms. *qui* to *que*, but unnecessarily; for constructions with relative *qui* followed by the subjunctive, see Moignet, 229.

894. W. supplies the missing object by correcting *chi* to *chis = chi les*; cf. also 906.

900. *Tut en brande* 'pitching perilously', not 'burning' as glossed by Gdf. 1, 721 and TL 1, 1120; see W. in *MLR* 21 (1929), 401–2.

901–2. 'And because of the storm it is touch-and-go whether the boat with them [in it] will capsize'.

913–14. Though the Ms. reading is comprehensible as it stands ('there was danger only from its teeth, and these [masc. in OF] were 1500'), it makes little or no sense in the context. What must have been the original hyperbolic vigour of the passage is preserved in the Latin prose translations, and can be restored by emending *out* to *oust*, following W., and *cil furent* to *sil fuïssent* (cf. W.'s *sil fuireient*). For a translation, see Intro., p. 21.

915–16. 'In addition to the waves which it caused, nothing more was needed to make a great storm' (W.).

920. *Ferat* being the only instance of the unreduced future of *faire* in our text (see Glossary), W. corrects to *en frat*.

928. *Le* is no doubt for *la*, i.e. the first monster.

950. Cf. note to l. 157.

958. All the examples of *estorse* in TL 3, 1424 relate to hunting, with the sense 'movement of prey to escape capture'.

968. *al secc* 'on to dry land', found both in Wace's *Brut* (ed. I. Arnold), l. 6814, and *Rou* II (ed. A. J. Holden), l. 6572.

1000. At this point in *NB* there are two other chapters, the first the Island of the Three Choirs (ch. 17) which has three groups of inhabitants, boys, men and old men, each group differently dressed and singing in turns. The third of the intruding monks remains here, forcing Benedeit in the *Voyage* to explain his disappearance rather enigmatically later on (1493–1504). In the other chapter omitted (ch. 18) a large bird drops a bunch of magnificent grapes into Brendan's lap, food which sustains them through a three-day fast. The omission of the two episodes allows Benedeit to maintain the quickening dramatic pace of his poem.

1003–4. 'if it had been the first [of the two], this peril would not [in their estimation] have been smaller [than the other], but would have been greater'. The poet is comparing the respective fearsomeness of the griffin and the sea-serpent. The second only seems lesser to them because of the experience of the first (W.).

1005–6. 'They are not afraid because their thoughts are turned to God, and [they are aware of] his protection'. W. interprets *defens* as 'prohibition'.

1007. The griffin was a fabulous animal usually represented as having the head and wings of an eagle and the body and hindquarters of a lion.

1011–14. 'There is no plank in the boat of such strength that the griffin cannot tear it away with a mere [blow of its] claw. The ship very nearly capsizes because of the very violence [of its flight] and the wind it creates'.

1025. *chaït* is recorded both as preterite and a past participle in OF. The former seems marginally preferable here.

1031–2. The feast-day of St Peter (and St Paul) is 29 June. Peter, according to a tradition dating from around A.D. 200, was put to death and buried on or near the site of the present Vatican basilica, also believed to be the site of Nero's gardens.

1044. TL 4, 743 accepts the sense of 'confusion' proposed for *guerre* by W., but with reservations.

1055. 'This danger has not yet happened to you'; i.e., the monks have taken fright when there is no danger.

1061. '. . . the service that was appropriate to the day'.

1064 ff. The Great Pillar and Canopy. This episode could call to mind the description of an iceberg; see Selmer, p. 90 n. 85. A similar episode in *Mael Duin*, closely paralleled by details in *Hui Corra*, refers to a silver column in the sea, eight oarstrokes in circumference, with a silver net coming out of the summit. A mesh of the net is taken to be offered on the altar of Armagh.

1065. *jargunce* 'jacinth'. The OED notes that among the ancients this was a gem of a blue colour, probably a sapphire. Hence in l. 1067 *saphire* is probably adjectival (W.).

1074. 'It could not have been made [even] for all the [wealth of the] world'; cf. Mod. Eng. 'to cost the earth'. The correction *uvrét* 1073 is W.'s from Ms. *B*.

1076. 'He finds the time long getting there'.

1084. *Ço* is the object: 'it (the beam) supported all this', i.e. *alter* 1079, *sacraires* 1081, *pavemenz* 1082.

1095–6. 'He is certain of not being unfaithful to (*lit*. turning away from) God, since he is taking it (the chalice) in order to serve him with it' (W.).

1103 ff. The Episode of the Smithy of Hell, paralleled in *Mael Duin* (ch. 21), has echoes of the island of the Cyclops in the *Aeneid*. Selmer (p. 90) suggests that the description represents the eruption of a volcano.

1132. For *féd* 'man', see B. Foster, 'Fé, fée and maufé' in *French Studies* 6 (1952), 345–52.

1156. *Trespasset* 'passes over' from Ms. *D* seems preferable, though W. corrects to *les passet*.

1166. In view of the apparently masc. gender of *isle* (cf. note to p. 489), both fem. *cuverte* and the form *fumé* (also 1170) make this line unsatisfactory grammatically as well as hypometric. W. corrects *aluminé* 1165 to *alumee*, and *fumé* to *fumee*. The sense emerges clearly from the text however it is edited.

1168. The misreading of *oent* as *cent*, and the repetition of *plusurs* from the end of the previous line are obvious scribal corruptions which we correct following W.

1170. *Fumé*, which we have again refrained from correcting, is probably for *fum*, which would give the line a correct syllable-count.

1173–6. These lines are Benedeit's own, though probably based partially on a commonplace; cf. *Roland* 1010–11: 'Pur sun seignor deit hom susfrir destreiz / E endurer e granz chalz e granz freiz' (repeated 1117–18). A further example of *plusur* with its original comparative force of 'more' is to be found at 1834 (cf. W.'s note to his l. 1840).

1183. *Lit.* 'there was no delay except until the morning when they saw . . .', in other words 'hardly had the next day dawned when . . .'. The usual expression is *ne demora . . . que*, but the conj., as here, can be omitted; cf. the examples quoted in TL 2, 1384–5.

1186. *Las = la les*: 'the wind brought them there'.

1191–2. The meaning of these lines (with no equivalent in *NB*) is not clear; *lit.* '[the mountain] does not slope down more [steeply] towards the shore than where it extends higher up'. W., who does not translate here, sees this as a description of the island 'as a cone, sloping evenly from bottom to top'.

1205–10. In *NB* the monks are later informed by Judas that this volcanic activity celebrates Hell's rejoicing at the engulfing of another damned soul (W.).

1210. 'Then sucks (*lit.* receives) them back in, for they belong to it (*lit.* are its own)'; this presupposes an Anglo-Norman rhyme [uə] : [yə].

1213–14. *Boche* (< *BOTTJA) 'hump' is Mod. Fr. *bosse*. The rhyme with *roche* might indicate a Norman or Picard dialectal pronunciation. Though there is no other example of this development in our text, the English loan-words *cherry*, *chive*, *fashion* (Fr. *cerise*, *cive*, *façon*) seem to show that it may not have been unkown in Anglo-Norman; cf. Pope § 1092.

1223. *Periz* is retained with the sense 'doomed, lost,'; cf. Marie de France, *Guigemar* (ed. Ewert), l. 67, and *Vie de Seint Auban* (ed. Harden), ll. 243, 465, 913. Two of the other Mss. have *pelfiz*, *pelfés* 'plucked bare'.

1228. We have kept *rosast* 'pushed back' with *o*; cf. TL 8, 1190 under *rëuser*.

1240. *Faldrat* 'will fail to take place'; cf. *Yvain* 5486 'La bataille ne puet faillir Ne remenoir en nule guise'.

1244. 'will there [ever] be any hour that I am out [of my torment]?'

1246. *crie* is a deliberative subjunctive: '. . . whether I am to cry for mercy.

1265 ff. Judas's account of his misdeeds is not derived from *NB* which has merely 'Ego sum infelicissimus Judas atque negotiator pessimus', p. 66. On Brendan's visit to Hell, cf. D. D. R. Owen, *The Vision of Hell: Infernal Journeys in Medieval Literature* (Edinburgh and London, 1970), 22–27, 59–62, 116–18.

1269. *pur* 'even to the point of'; cf. *Roland* 514, 3617 and G. Moignet's note to this last line in his edition (Paris 1969, p. 254).

1273–5. The object of *celoue* 1275 is *offrande* 1273 and l. 1274 is to be taken as a parenthesis: 'he exhorted [that] it [should] all [be given] to the poor'.

1279. 'denied comfort (goods) to God's poor'. It is difficult to understand how W. in his glossary could construe *bien* as an adverb here.

1285–6. There is no *que* in 1285, a further example of parataxis, and in 1286 the paratactical construction is compounded by ellipsis of the finite verb.

1303. The notion of a respite for the damned is probably of Jewish origin according to P. F. Baum, 'Judas' Sunday Rest', *MLR* 18 (1923), 168–82, who notes two other examples of Judas's relief in OF literature, *Baudouin de Sebourc* and *Esclarmonde*. In Christian legend the respite came about through the intercession of St Michael and St Paul; cf. D. D. R. Owen, *The Vision of Hell*, pp. 307, 51–5.

1307. The passage is more precise in *NB*: 'from Christmas until Epiphany'.

1309. *NB* makes it clear that the feasts involved here are: 'Purificacione Dei Genitricis [2 Feb.] atque Assumpcione [15 Aug.]'.

1314. According to TL 3, 646, there is no other recorded example of *entrebat* 'interruption'.

1321. W.'s correction to *E es peines* involves a clumsy repetition with the previous line. It might however be possible to interpret Ms. *espeines* as an unattested substantive formed on OF *espeneïr* 'expiate (sins)' (cf. TL 3, 1176–7), and a correct syllable-count can be obtained simply by omitting the conj. *e*, the force of which is in any case unclear in W.'s text. As for *en turmentes* of the previous line (corrected by W. to *es turmentes*), cf. *en tenebres* 1418, *en estals* 708. The rhyming of identical words in ll. 1321–2 is found only twice elsewhere in our text: 1259 and 1375. W. (p. lvii) points out that the addition of the preceding syllable in each case produces normal leonine rhymes.

1324. Sc. *li fius a*[s] *dïables* 'the devils' domain'.

1334. '[They believe] that others in comparison with them suffer no torture'. W. prefers the word-order of the other Mss.: *Que altre vers eals mal . . .*

1337. 'There is no one [who] has more than one of the two.'

1354. On infernal wheels, see D. D. R. Owen, *op. cit.*, pl. 1 and *passim*.

1377–8. '. . . as if it had lain ten years in fire blown by bellows'.

1383–6. 'And no marble is so hard that it would not have melted had it been put on [the fire]'. The next two lines (1385–6) are badly corrupt in the Ms. W. corrects *nuls* to *mis*, following the other Mss., and translates: 'I am made for (or adapted to) this wrath . . ., for my body is unable to perish'. Cf. the Latin prose translation: 'Set ego miser, quicquid patiar, adnichilari non possum'.

1409–10. The rhyme *beivre* : *quivre* is repeated at 1421–2 where the spelling is *quivere*. W. corrects in both instances to *queivre* to reflect the rhyme in [ejvrə]. Though Latin CŪPREUM gives *cuivre* in French, other dialectal variants of the word with *ei* are attested in OF; cf. Fouché, *op. cit.* ii, 405; Pope § 1196.

1412. Strict observance of the flexional endings of OF would make *mals* the obj. of the verb and *li altre* (sc. devils) its subject.

1420. W. interprets the construction *ne guarder quant* as a variant of the more usual *ne guarder l'eure que* (cf. TL 4, 149–50); *lit.*: I do not look for the moment when my heart might burst', that is, 'I am in constant fear that . . .'.

1428. Medieval time of day was, of course, based on the canonical hours. *Nune* here must have its etymological sense of 'the ninth hour' (i.e. mid-afternoon, nine hours after *prime* at 6 a.m.). It was only subsequently, because of the imprecision inherent in this sort of measurement of time, and because the ninth hour was a recognised meal-time, that it came in English to mean 'noon'. See W. Rothwell, 'The hours of the day in medieval French' in *French*

Studies 13 (1960), 240–51, and 'A further note on *nonne*', *ibid.* 20 (1966), 223–5.

1430. OF *eneveies* 'soon' appears in Beroul's *Tristan* both as *anevois* and *enevoies* (ed. Ewert, 2441, 3051), though the four-syllable form seems indicated here by the metre (W.).

1440. 'at the fact that'.

1442. *deit*: cf. note to l. 504.

1447–8. 'The good and evil [that I have performed in my lifetime] are now clear to me, [and I understand] which [of the two] were closer to (*lit.* dearer in) [my] heart'.

1452. *Nie* is most probably a pres. suj. (< NĔCEM) with analogical final *e* for *z*: 'so that I do not drown'. The Ms. spelling *neie*, emended here for the sake of the rhyme, is a wholly analogical form reflecting the stem of the infin. *neiier* (Mod. Fr. *noyer*), and the vocalic alternation *ei/i* of its pres. indic. paradigm.

1456. 'Since it was not bought with my own money' (W.).

1457–62. *NB* is more specific in stating that the rock to which Judas clung was the actual stone which he had once placed across a ditch for public safety (W.).

1471. The sense of *calengent* seems from the context to be 'claim defiantly' though we have not found another example with a similar construction.

1476. 'Their efforts are futile in the end'. For this sense of *a l'estorse*, see TL 3, 1424 (cf. Gdf. 3, 628). W. translates 'in the snatching away' (cf. l. 958 and note above).

1478. 'There is no demon to whom this is not very irksome.'

1492. *agreies* 'equipment'. This is the only example cited by TL 1, 214, but other forms also derived from Old Norse *greiða* 'make ready, equip' are found: *agroi*, *agroier*, TL 1, 214, and *groie*, TL 4, 684. Cf. *Anglo-Norman Dictionary* (1, 17) where the word is wrongly glossed from Ms. *D* s.v. *agree* and lacking s.v. *agrei*.

1493–1504. Benedeit is forced to add this brief episode to explain the disappearance of the third of the intruding monks; cf. note to l. 1000.

1510. 'no one except myself'. This periphrastic use of *cors* for the personal pronoun is common in OF; cf. for ex. *Roland* 525, 892, 1984 etc.

1514. Benedeit does not explain that the rock, *bodme*, contains the life-giving fountain mentioned in 1585; cf. *NB* pp. 74–7.

1515 ff. It was not unusual in Irish hagiography for saints to visit one another; cf. Selmer, p. 91 n. 92. The real Brendan visited St Columba on Iona some time after 563.

1518. The periphrastic construction *estre savant* has the same meaning as the simple verb *saveir*.

1526. 'shows [it] to them'.

1528. Generally in OF, the third person pronoun retains the weak form, not the strong as here, even when following the verb; cf. Moignet, 131–2.

1537. Paul, known as the first hermit, took up the solitary life in the Egyptian desert during the persecution of the emperor Decius (249–51). His life was written by St Jerome (ed. J.-P. Migne, *Patrologia latina* XXIII, coll. 17–28). In the *Brendan* legend the desert is replaced by a more appropriate lonely island.

1543. 'according to my limited ability'.

1546. 'he has given me more credit for my service than I deserve' (*lit*. he has counted it to me at more than it is worth) (W.).

1549 ff. The motif of a ship ready to transport a voyager and sailing under invisible guidance is widespread and is found elsewhere in OF literature, e.g. Marie de France, *Guigemar* (cf. Ewert's note to his edition, p. 165).

1551. *Cunduit* is preterite despite its form without *s*.

1568–9. 'No [week] ever passed (*lit*. was ever empty) without its bringing me three fish'.

1574. 'He through whom this happened was Lord indeed!'

1582. 'He did not do so (fail to return) out of reluctance or [because] he despised me'; cf. OF *sor son pois* 'against his will', TL 7, 1337 (also 9, 916).

1648. 'His (Adam's) heirs' refers to the mariners.

1674. Sc. *de quel materie il seit faiz*. The rhyme *veire* : *materie* seems to presuppose a form of the latter [matejrə]; cf. note to l. 53 above.

1681 ff. These lines are based on Revelation 21: 19–20: 'And the foundations of the wall were garnished with all manner of precious stones. The first foundation was jasper . . .'. On the symbolic virtues of such stones, see for example *Anglo-Norman Lapidaries* (eds. P. Studer and J. Evans, Paris, 1924) (W.).

1695–1700. The wall enclosing Paradise is established on a mountain of gold, which is itself on hills of marble raised high above the sea (W.).

1699. *Esteit* is not the impf. indic. of *estre*, but the pres. indic. of *ester*, 'stands'.

1702. '. . . into which we ought to have entered (*lit*. which should have been frequented by us)', if, that is, Adam's heirs had not been exluded.

1703 ff. The description is an addition of the poet, who may have relied on Genesis and Revelation for his inspiration; cf. Revelation 21: 12: 'and at the gates twelve angels'; Genesis 3: 24: 'So he drove out the man; and he placed at the east of the garden of Eden Cherubims, and a flaming sword which turned every way to keep the way of the tree of life' (W.).

1707–8. The two semi-learned forms *glavies* : *savies* no doubt rhyme in [ajvəs]; cf. the spelling *glaive* 1725, and the note to l. 53 above. *Savie* appears alongside *saive* in the *Roland* (cf. 20 and 248). Cf. also *munies* 107 for *muines*.

1733–8. 'The meadow, which is constantly in flower, is a garden. The flowers there smell very sweet, fitting for the place where the pious live, [a place that is] a delight of trees and flowers, a priceless spot of fruit and sweet scents'. *Cum* 1736: 'as befits'.

1746. In order to complete the sense, it is necessary to repeat *tuz dis i est* from the preceding line. Similarly *i sunt* must be understood in 1747 and *i sunt repleni(z)* in 1748 (W.).

1749–53. The description of the land as flowing with milk and honey, an embroidery by Benedeit on his source, is a clear reference to the Old Testament Book of Exodus. In his introduction to his German translation of our poem, E. Ruhe argues that Benedeit in fact deliberately portrays Brendan as a new Moses-figure leading God's chosen people to the Promised Land (*ed. cit.*, 22 ff.).

1751–2. Though the actual forms *ruseie* (*rosoie*) and *ruseit* (*rosé*) appear to be unique, the corresponding masc. *rosoi* and fem. *rosee* are common in OF.

1754. Our correction is independent of the other Mss., each of which has a different reading here. A further emendation of *grande pere* to *granz peres* would give better sense ('There are no such large gems in [any] treasure') and a correct syllable-count. Cf. W.'s note to his l. 1760, and l. 316 above.

1760. W. corrects to *Ne dunt mals vent* 'nor whence evil comes'. We retain the Ms. reading (except to emend *nel* to *ne*) and understand 'nor will he experience ill winds', though this is far from clear.

1768. Ms. *Lur le*. W.'s conviction that each and every line must be syllabically perfect leads him to postulate what the recognises himself as being an inadmissible enclisis: *urel = ure li*.

1773. The common meaning of *diviser (OF deviser)* is 'divide, divide up', here used figuratively 'describe in detail'; cf. *divisiuns* 1778 'explanations'.

1776. *ciprés* might be read *ci prés*, but this does not seem to make good sense in the context. It must be admitted, none the less, that neither TL nor Gdf. give *ciprés* in such a simile or metaphor.

1783. *prendre* 'understand, grasp' could represent an instance of the omission of a prefix but more probably the verb has simply taken on the wider sense (W.).

1801. The subject of the first clause would seem to be the celestial guide, that of the second Brendan.

1817. 'It is not only the families who are glad, but . . .'.

1824. The difficulty of taking *quanque* as an adjective could be avoided by an emendation suggested by Professor T. B. W. Reid: *Quanqu'al busuign a Deu ruvat* 'whatever in his need he asked of God'.

Glossary

The Glossary is intended to be complete, including all words in the text and their meanings, though not necessarily all inflected forms; regular forms of verbs of the first and second conjugations are, for example, excluded in most cases and only the infinitive given. Proper names are listed separately in the Index of Proper Names. The line-references are exhaustive except where the contrary is indicated by the use of '*etc.*'. Where there is more than one form of a word, the entry is under the most frequent spelling, though cross-references are given in most instances. The letter '*n*' after a reference indicates that this line figures in the Notes to the text.

Nouns are normally listed under the singular oblique form, and adjectives under the masculine singular oblique. Other forms are identified. Pronouns and definite articles appear under their nominative singular form. Genders are given for nouns and adjectives only if guaranteed by text or context. Verbs are listed under the infinitive which is followed immediately by a line-reference if the form itself occurs in the text. So-called irregular verbs have all forms given, but in cases where there is one form only, the entry is made under this form. Pronominal verbs (*v. pron.*) are distinguished from those that are properly reflexive (*v. refl.*) or reciprocal (*v. recipr.*).

a[1] 22, 34, 46 *etc.*, (*with article*) **al** 120, 131, 163 *etc.*, **as** 146, 185, 229 *etc.*, **a** (= **as**) 338, 806, 1324; *prep.* (*loc.*) to 163, 193*n*, 267 *etc.*; at 338, 657, 826 *etc.*; from 242; in, on 262, 423, 450 *etc.*; (*temporal*) at 575, 618, 627 *etc.*; for 183, 605, 996, 1793; on 328, 400, 405 *etc.*; in 628, 1183*n*, 1304 *etc.*; to 555; *see also* **desque**; (*indir.obj.*) to 34, 46, 74 *etc.*; of 145, 401, 1824; for 351, 640, 746 *etc.*; from 1278, 1714, 1790; in 806; (*possessive*) of 131; (*final*) in, on, for 22, 260, 753 *etc.*; (*verb* + **a** + *inf.*) *following* **aler fors** 218, **aveir** 613, **estre** 300, **ester** 1769, **prendre** 284, 501, 596; (*modal*) with 930, 1142, 1160 *etc.*; in 189, 387, 1037 *etc.*; according to 993; *cf. also* **a celét** 807, **a curs entrin** 1639, **a dreit curs** 1663, **a nul desrei** 302, **a lur espeir** 381, **a force** 1475, **a plain, plein** 210, 598, **a plentét** 293, **a plus** 1546, **a soüt**

373, **a tart** 635, 1139; (*instrumental*) with 377, 620, 860 *etc*.; on 1590; at 995; by 1202, 1726; (*material*) of 273, 681; (*other uses*) *cf*. **entrer** 193*n*, **failir** 787, 1494, **fort** 626, 896, **num** 280, **rost** 1373, **savant** 1788

a², *interj*. ah! 454, 1239
abeïe, *sf*. abbey 671, 693
abét 152, 338, 651 *etc*., **abéth** 13, 89; *nom. sg*. **abes** 32, 39, 86 *etc*.; *sm*. abbot
abit *see* **habit**
abööter; *v.a*. look out for 884
abraser; *v.n*. blaze, burn vigorously 1683
absolud *see* **jusdi**
acaliz, *pp.adj.nom.sg.m*. numbed, stupefied 1360
acater; *v.a*. buy 1450
achant, *s*.: **prendre a**. capsize 1014
aclore; *ind.pr*. 3 **aclot** 1645; *pp.f*. **aclose** 253; *v.a*. surround, enclose
ad *see* **aveir**
adamant, *s*. diamond 1713
adenter; *v.n*. capsize, overturn 902
adés, *adv*. without stopping 188; at once 377
ados, *s*. support 80
adubez, *pp.adj.obl.pl*. set, adorned 677
aësmer; *v.a*. consider, judge 1050
aëz *see* **aveir**
afamét, *sm.nom.pl*. hungry, famished 795
agnel, *sm*. lamb 1282
agreger 696, 1352, *v.a*. make solemn 696; exacerbate 1352
agreies, *sf. pl*. equipment 1492*n*
ahan 380, 1314, **han** 546, *sm*. fatigue 380; torment, suffering 546, 1314
aiez, aient *see* **aveir**
aigre 941, 1024, **egre** 788, *adj*. bitter, harsh 788; sharp, violent 941; fierce 1024
aigue 332, 704, 1457 *etc*., **eigue** 997, *sf*. water 332, 704, 997 *etc*.; stream 1457

ailurs 88, 1111, 1203, **ailur** 746, *adv*. elsewhere
aines, *s*.: **pendre en a**. dangle 1711
ainxe, *s*. anxiety 1175
ainz 61, 118, 198 *etc*., **enz** 427, 1004; *prep*. before 427; *adv*. before, previously 848, 988; *conj*. rather 198, 469, 954 *etc*.; instead 1298; **a. . . . que** before 118, 616, 617 *etc*.
ainzjurnals, *adj.f.pl*. (conducted) before dawn 576
air, *sm*. air 497, 1019, 1129 *etc*.; atmosphere 971, 1345; sky 255, 1007, 1757
aïr, *sm*. violence 1013*n*
aise, *s*.: **faire a**. bring comfort, relief 986
ajurner; *v.impers*. break (*of day*) 1485
al *see* **a**
alçur, *adj*. lofty 279
aleger 1351, *v.a*. alleviate
aler¹ 160, 231, 670 *etc*.; *ind.pr.1* **voi** 1316, 1358, **vois** 432, *2* **vas** 1322, *3* **vait** 153, 157, 349 *etc*., *5* **alez** 363, *6* **vunt** 210, 218, 266 *etc*.; *fut*. 2 **iras** 1595, *3* **irat** 141, *5* **irez** 770; *impf. ind.6* **alouent** 665, 1131; *pret.3* **alat** 84, 161, 317 *etc*., *6* **alerent** 287, 1163; *impf.subj.3* **alast** 612; *imper.2* **va** 424, 773, *4* **alum** 1092, *5* **alez** 285; *pp*. **alét** 669; *v.n*. go 160, 231, 287 *etc*.; proceed, continue 141, 161, 706 *etc*.; depart, leave 153; walk, journey 665, 1511; head (for) 436; travel 439; sail 631; move 1149; spread 1815; *v.a*. (*aux. aveir*) walk 669*n*; (+ *inf*.) go (and) 84, 285, 308 *etc*.; (+ *gerund*; *expressing purpose or duration*) 363, 833, 1059; **a. la veie** follow, proceed along a path 266; **en a**. depart, go off 770, 1801; go 349, 432, 1322 *etc*.; be used up 758*n*; extend 1750; **a. fors** set forth 218; **a. avant** proceed, go further 1729, 1787; go in front 1775; **s'en a**. *v.pron*. depart, leave,

go away 157, 210, 370 *etc.*; **s'en a.**
avant move on 1029, 1181, 1487;
cf. **alment**
aler² 232*n*, *v.a.* haul
aleür, *s.* passage, footwalk 1671
alis, *adj.pl.* unleavened 410
alment, *sm.* going 144
almoine, *s.* alms 1449
aloeces, *adv.*: **ci a.** to this (very) place
173; *cf.* **ileoc**
alques, *adv.*: **a. de** something of, to a
certain degree 1454
alte *see* **halt**
alter, *sm.* altar 1079
altre, *adj.* another 402, 431, 927 *etc.*;
other 517, 1066, 1313 *etc.*; previous 824, 1616; *pron.* other 171,
283, 644 *etc.*; **a. rien** anything else
485
altretant, *adv.* as long 1348
alumer 326, *v.a.* light
aluminé, *pp.adj.* aflame 1165
amasser; *v.n.* unite, solidify 1155;
pp.adj. solid 679; heaped up 1662
ambes, *adj.f.pl.* both 204, 1662
amedous, *adj.m.pl.* both 1338
amener; *subj.pr.3* **amenget** 1520; *v.a.*
guide s.o.'s steps 725; bring along
1520
amer; *v.a.* love 566, 730
amertét, *s.* bitter affliction, torment
740
amestistes, *s.pl.* amethysts 676, 1687
amis, *sm.nom.sg.* friend 46, 395
amonester; *v.a.* admonish, give warn-
ing 223
ample, *adj.* great 38
amunt, *prep.* up (*of watercourse*) 487,
855; *adv.* up 1192*n*, 1232, 1399
etc.; upstream 637; **a. aval** back
and forth 259, 550*n*
amur, *s.* love 70, 1269
an¹ 379, 545, 551 *etc.*; *obl.pl.* **anz**
719, 736, 874 *etc.*; *sm.* year
an² *see* **en**
anceis, *adv.* before 532, 561, 1597
angel 140; *nom.pl.* **angele** 519; *obl.pl.*
angeles 100; *sm.* angel

angelïel, *adj.* angelic 1531
anguisus, *adj.* full of anguish 1424
annuier; *ind.impf.3* **ennuiout** 1579;
subj.pr.3 **anuit** 1387, **annuit** 1478;
v.a. and n.(impers.) trouble 1387,
1579; be irksome to 1478*n*
annüus, *adj.* unfavourable, stormy
972
anquist, *pret.3 of* **anquerre**, *v.a.*
inquire, ask about 413
antaile, *s.* opening *or* carving 1677
anuit,¹ *adv.* tonight 425, 1434, 1436
anuit² 1387 *see* **annuier**
aorber; *v.a.* blind 1649
apaiser 1270; *v.a.* reconcile 1270;
pacify 1722
aparceut 335, **aparçout** 1137, *pret.3*
of **aparceivre**, *v.a.* see, realise 335;
v.pron. become aware (of) 1137
apareil, *s.* preparation (*for journey*)
106
apareiler; *v.a.* make ready 828
apeler; *v.a.* call 164, 808, 1517; call
on, invoke 889
aporter; *v.a.* bring 301, 1565
aporteür, *s.* supplier, porter 744
apostoiles, *sm.nom.sg.* missionary,
envoy 8*n*
apostorie, *sm.* pope 1034
apparut, *pret.3 of* **appareir**, *v.n.*
appear 724, 1103
aprendre; *fut.2* **aprendras** 1793; *pp.*
apris 733; *v.a.* teach 733; *v.n.* learn
1793
aprés, *adv.* after, following behind
187, 1775; *prep.* after 981
apresmer 1252; *ind.pr.6* **aprisment**
1644, 1655; *ind.impf.3* **apresmout**
1253, 1463, **aprismout** 917; *v.a.*
917; *v.n.* 1252, 1253, 1644, 1655;
v.n. (impers.) 1463; approach
apresser; *v.a.* threaten, beset 1002
aprester; *v.a.* prepare 1629
arbeleste, *s.* crossbow 1151
arbre, *sf.* tree 489*n*, 494, 554 *etc.*;
wood, timber 274
ardeir 1382; *ind.pr.3* **art** 1138, 1157,
1159 *etc.*, 6 **ardent** 1706; *v.n.* burn;

pres.part.adj. **ardant** 788, 1404, *pl.* **ardanz** 1124, 1128, 1208, burning 1124 *etc.*; parching 788

arere, *adv.* back 932, 1228, 1597; ahead, afterwards 547

argent, *s.* silver 291

ariver 964, *v.n* land, come to shore 386n, 483, 854 *etc.*

armer 1212, *v.a.* arm

armes, *s.pl.* military strength 5

arsun, *s.* burning 757

art[1] *see* **ardeir**

art,[2] *s.* skill 33

as = a + les; *see* **a**[1]

asart, *sm.* clearing 1158

aseeir; *pret.3* **asist** 282, 511, 1692; *imper.5* **aseez** 452; *pp.* **asis** 50, 734, 870, *f.* **asise** 499, 1036; *v.a.* set, place 50; establish 734, 1036; set (*of gems*) 1692; *v.n. and refl.* sit (down) 282, 452, 870; *pp.adj.* occupied, covered 499

asembler; *v.refl.* gather 729

asen, *s.* teaching, instruction 581

asener 474; *subj.pr.3* **asent** 506; *v.a.* teach, instruct 474, 506, 1772

asens, *sm.* indication of direction 786; guidance 1540

asez, *adv.* enough, sufficient 301, 366, 415 *etc.*

asis(e), **asist** *see* **aseeir**

asolt, *ind.pr.3 of* **asoldre**, *v.a.* absolve 346

asorber; *v.n.* lose one's sight 1650

asoür, *adj.* confident, assured 839

asperir 1316, *v.n.* undergo torment 1316

aspirer; *v.a.* inspire 142

ast 825, 857, **ast vos**, **vus** 188, 310, 356 *etc.*, *interj.* look! behold!

at *see* **aveir**

atendre; *ind.pr.1* **atent** 1555, *3* **atent** 338, *6* **atendent** 1626; *fut.2* **atendras** 1798; *subj.impf.1* **attendisse** 1548; *imper.2* **atent** 454; *v.a.* wait for

atraire 173, *v.a.* bring, haul

atre, *sm.* holy place, enclosure 718

aturner; *v.a.* turn, resort (to) 1180

aürer; *v.a.* worship 1287

aüverz, *pp.adj.* open 1206

aval, *prep.* down 172; *adv.* down 1709; *see also* **amunt**

avaler 868; *v.n.* fly down

avant, *prep.* before 171; *adv.* onward, further on 1029, 1063, 1181 *etc.*; further, more 1262; forward 1468, 1517, 1524 *etc.*; in front 1775; beyond, further on 1792; **a. de** beyond, further than 1786

avei, *sm.* guidance 581

aveier; *v.a.* guide 140

aveir 62, 63, 80 *etc.*; *ind.pr.1* **ai** 749, 1310, 1314 *etc.*, *2* **as** 1318, 1321, 1596 *etc.*, *3* **ad** 9, 53, 109 *etc.*, at 258, 286, 316 *etc.*, *4* **avum** 127, 192, 415, *5* **avez** 468, 546, 563 *etc.*, *6* **unt** 70, 371, 373 *etc.*; *fut.1* **avrai** 1430, 1432, *3* **avrat** 25, 199, 1482 *etc.*, *5* **averez** 227, 585, *6* **avrunt** 66; *ind.impf.1* **aveie** 1543, 1570, *3* **aveit** 36, 167, 1083 *etc.*, *6* **aveient** 182; *pret.1* **oi** 1284, 1297, 1563 *etc.*, *2* **ous** 1598, *3* **out** 75, 76, 78 *etc.*, *5* **oustes** 1117, *6* **ourent** 240, 856, 1196; *subj.pr.3* **ait** 226, 1140, 1337 *etc.*, *5* **aiez** 366, *6* **aient** 650; *subj.impf.3* **oust** 913, *4* **ousum** 764, *6* **oussent** 655; *imper.5* **aiez** 803, 1501, **aëz** 361; *pp.* **oüt** 468, **oüd** 1484; *v.a.* have, possess 25, 62, 63 *etc.*; hold, consider 962, 1582; get back, recover 1196; (+ a + *inf.*) have to 613, 614; *v.aux.* 9, 109, 124 *etc.*; *v.n.(impers.)* 53, 672 *etc.*, (*with* **i**) 135, 184, 258 *etc.*, there is, are; *subst. inf.* money 1271

avenir; *ind.pr.3* **avient** 241; *fut.3* **avendrat** 196; *v.n.* happen (to), befall 196, 241

averer 954; *v.a.* confirm

aviruns, *s.pl.* oars 229

avisiün, *s.* vision 1777

aviver; *v.n.* intensify 970

avolst, *pret.3 of* **avoldre**, *v.a.* cover, line 176n

bailis, *sm.nom.sg.* steward 452
bainer; *v.a.* bathe 827
baïs, *adj.nom.sg.m.* waiting expect-
antly 615
baiser 660, 1269, *v.a.* kiss 153, 660,
1269 *etc.*; *v.refl.* kiss one another
607, 691
baldorie, *sf.* joy 542
banc, *sm.* bench, seat 282
barge, *sf.* boat 620
bas, *adv.* low 521, 1039; **basse**, *adj.f.*
low 1263
bat[1] 886; *nom.sg.* **baz** 600; *sm.* boat
bat,[2] *ind.pres.3 of* **batre**, *v.n.* beat, lap
1696
bataile, *sf.* battle 945, 1019
beal 443, 1554, **bel** 695, 1716;
nom.sg. **beals** 1628, **bel** 268; *obl.pl.*
beals 82, 1731, **beus** 500; *f.sg.* **bele**
292, 671, 840; *adj.* beautiful (*physical*) 268, 292, 500 *etc.*; handsome
1716; splendid 840, 1628; fine
443, 695, (*of weather*) 1554;
(*address*) good 1039, 1535; *adv.*
beal beautifully, splendidly 1734;
bel sweetly 512
bein *see* **bien**
beitrer 233, *v.n.* steer
beivre 804, 1409, 1422, 1578;
ind.pr.3 **beit** 1587; *ind.impf.3*
beveit 811; *v.a.* drink; *subst.inf.*
beivre 290, 357, 603 *etc.*
bel *see* **beal**
ben *see* **bien**
berbiz, *sf.pl.* sheep 387, 399, 417
beril, *sm.* beryl 1085, 1690
beste, *sf.* creature, animal 924, 927,
933; sea-creature 1058; great fish
or whale 469, 552, 880
betumeit, *s.* bog, damp ground 802*n*
beus 500 *see* **beal**
bien 53, 143, 152 *etc.*, **ben** 23, **bein**
34, *adv.* well 202, 266, 601 *etc.*;
well, for sure (*esp. with* **saveir**) 23,
766, 795 *etc.*; clearly 143, 196,
300, 313 *etc.*; faithfully, steadfastly
34, 152, 1502; firmly 53, 964
1200; richly 676; indeed 928, 960,

1146 *etc.*; completely 1407; enjoy-
ing plain sailing, out of danger
1822; (+ *adj. or adv.*) very 430,
438, 480 *etc.*; **mult b. avant** a good
distance forward 1771; *s.* comfort
1279*n*; good, good action 1446,
1447; *see also* **propre**
bienfaiz, *s.pl.* acts of kindness 1606
bis, *adj.* grey, dark 262
blanc 699; *nom.sg.m.* **blancs** 1675;
obl.pl.m. **blancs** 499, **blanz** 410;
f.sg. **blanche** 388, 490, 849, **blance**
1533; *adj.* white; *s.* white (colour)
492
blasmer 16, *v.a.* reproach 1049
blef, *adj.* pale 264
boche, *sf.* hump, projection 1213*n*
bodme, *sf.* rock 1514*n*
bofs *see* **buf**
bois, *s.* wood, woodland 77, 1541,
1731, 1747
bon 13, 215, 362 *etc.*; *nom.sg.m.* **bons**
186, 1054, 1628; *f.* **bone** 292, 671,
1242; *adj.* good 13, 76, 82 *etc.*;
favourable 186, 215, 622; *sm.pl.*
the just 62; wants, desires 1763
bord, *s.* plank, timber 1011*n*
bovin, *adj.* of an ox 176
braiet, *ind.pr.3 of* **braier**, *v.n.* bellow
912
braist, *pret.3 of* **braire**, *v.n.* roar 930
branche, *sf.* branches 850
brancheie, *sf.* branches 496
brande, *s.*: **en b.** pitching perilously
900*n*
bretache, *s.* brattice, defensive parapet 1672
broche, *s.* spit 1365
brüere, *s.* heather 1158
buche[1] 908 *see* **busche**
buche,[2] *sf.* mouth 1452
buf 597; *obl.pl.* **bofs** 1146; *sm.* ox
buil, *ind.pr.1 of* **buillir**, *v.n.* boil 1371
buntét, *sf.* kindness 1545
burses, *s.pl.* purse 1275
busche 449, 999, **buche** 908, *sf.*
firewood
busuign 1824; *nom.sg.* **busuinz** 241;

obl.pl. **busuinz** 1629; *sm.* need, want

buter; *v.a.* push 486

buz, *s.pl.* butts, thrusts 1021

c' *see* **ço**

ça, *adv.* in this direction 1112; here to this place 1540; **ça avant** beyond, further on 1792

cacher; *v.a.* impel 1116

caçout *see* **chacer**

calcedoine, *s.* chalcedony 1082, 1685n

cald 1409; *nom.sg.m.* **calz** 754, 1345; *obl.pl.* **calz** 1174, 1425, **chalz** 1761; *adj.* hot 754, 1345, 1409; *s.* heat 1174, 1425, 1761

caldere, *s.* cauldron 835

calenger; *v.a.* claim defiantly 1471n

calin, *sm.* fog 1104, 1644, 1649 *etc.*

candeile, *s.* candle, light 324

cant 556, 558, **chant** 575; *sm.* hymn 556, 558; **c. de gals** cockcrow 575

canter *see* **chanter**

capitel, *s.* chapter-house 125

cardunt, *s.* thistle 1739

carn *see* **charn**

carnalment, *adv.* in the flesh 1795

caruine, *s.* rotting flesh 1106

castel, *sm.* castle 267

ceals *see* **cil**

ceil *see* **cel**

ceine, *sf.* Last Supper 393n, 1611; Easter Communion 829, 877

cel(e) *see* **cil**

cel 25, 140, 1278 *etc.*, **ceil** 520; *sm.* heaven

celebrïer; *v.a.* celebrate 843

celer; *ind.impf.1* **celoue** 1275; *v.a.* hide 198, 1275, 1277

celestïel, *adj.* heavenly 1532

celét, *s.*: **a c.** secretly 807

celui *see* **cil**

cent 1202, 1592, 1791, **cenz** 78, 800, 914; *adj.num.* one hundred

cerne, *s.*: **tut a c.** all around 869

cers, *sm.pl.* stags 390

certe, *adj.f.* certain 1620, 1728

certement, *adv.* clearly, with certainty 143; truly 1259

ces *see* **cist**

cesser; *v.n.* cease 1001, 1330; fail 224n

cest(e), cestui *see* **cist**

ceu, *adj.* dark 1392

cez *see* **cist**

chacer; *ind.impf.3* **caçout** 1015; *v.a.* pursue 1015; force, drive 985

chaër; *ind.pr.3* **cheot** 1156, **cheit** 1157; *pret.3* **chaït** 1025n, 4 **chaïmes** 521; *subj.pr.5* **chaiez** 818; *v.n.* fall 521, 1025, 1156, 1157; lapse 818

chaines, *s.pl.* chains 865n

chaitis, *adj.nom.sg.m.* wretched 1338, 1355

chaliz, *sm.* chalice 1093

chalz *see* **cald**

changer; *v.a.* change 1351

chant *see* **cant**

chanter; **canter** 853; *ind.impf.3* **chantout** 1037; *v.n.* sing 1037, 1039, 1057, 1061; *v.a.* sing, celebrate 569, 712, 1088; *subst.inf.* singing 853

chanud 825, **chanut** 407, *adj.* white(haired)

charger; *v.a.* load 887; command 136; fill 1654; *v.n.* bear fruit 1743; **chargét** *pp.adj.* laden 886

charn 447, **carn** 1557, *s.* meat 447; flesh 1557; *cf.* **os²**

chascun, checun *see* **chescun**

chef, *sm.* head (*of stream*) 489

cheit *see* **chaër**

cheles, *interj.* come now! tell me! 343

chemin, *sm.* way 1658, 1664

cheot *see* **chaër**

cher 160, 1819, **chier** 1448; *adj.* dear 962, 1039, 1535 *etc.*; worthy 160, 771; **aveir c.** cherish 962

chere, *sf.* mood, look 1284

chernel, *s.* crenel, parapet 1671

chescun 551, 745 *etc.*, **checun** 297, 872, **chascun** 750, 875; *nom.sg.m.* **chescuns** 884, **chescun** 692, **chas-**

cuns 1774; *f.* **chescune** 388, **chas-cun'** 1041; *pron.* each one 297, 388, 692, 750 *etc.*; *adj.* each 551, 745 *etc.*

chi *see* **qui**

chier *see* **cher**

chil 885 *see* **cil**

chis 1692 = **qui** + **les**

choisir 1189; *v.a.* see, distinguish 465, 849, 1668

chose 1195, **cose** 503, *s.* thing 503; **pur quel c.** why 1195

ci *see* **ici**

cil, *nom.sg.m.* 17, 18, 42 *etc.*, **icil** 165, 1133, **chil** 885; *obl.sg.m.* **cel** 49, 95, 97 *etc.*, **celui** 314; *nom.pl.m.* **cil** 121, 287, 537, **icil** 67, 910, 1029; *obl.pl.m.* **iceals** 28, 709, 1139, **ceals** 1286, 1332, **iceols** 123; *f.sg.* **cele** 890, 1542, 1652 *etc.*, **icele** 383, 1075; *neut.* **cel** 60, 117, 128; *demonstr.pron.* he, they, that (man), one 17, 18, 42 *etc.*; it 60*n*; the one 1343, 1344, 1345 *etc.*; the former, the first (*cf.* **cist**) 1445, 1605, 1775; this reason 117*n*; **cil e cil** both parties 607; **cil ... cil** this one ... that one 1024; *demonstr.adj.* that, those 28, 49, 75 *etc.*

cinc, *adj.num.* five 914

cinquante, *adj.num.* fifty 1591

ciprés, *s.* cypress tree 1776*n*

cire, *s.* wax 758

cirge, *s.* candle 326

cisler; *v.n.* blow, howl 94*n*

cist, *nom.sg.m.* 27, 86, 104 *etc.*, **icist** 19, 1004; *obl.sg.m.* **cest** 24, 30, 331 *etc.*, **icest** 726, 1534, **cestui** 171; *nom.pl.m.* **cist** 1108; *obl.pl.m.* **icez** 1256; *f.sg.* **ceste** 929, 931, **icest'** 1601; *f.pl.* **ces** 390*n*, **cez** 1799, **icez** 399; *demonstr.pron.* he, they, this (man) 86*n*, 104, 171 *etc.*; this one 1055; this 1303; the last mentioned, the latter (*cf.* **cil**) 1440, 1775; the second one 929, 931; *demonstr.adj.* this, these 19, 24, 27 *etc.*; this last 1004

citét, *sf.* city 278

clair *see* **cler**

clamer; *v.a.*: **c. culpe** make confession 1056

clarté 275, **clartét** 1691, *s.* brilliance 275; reflected light 1691

cler 579 *etc.*, **clair** 498, 1758; *f.* **clere** 481 *etc.*, **cler'** 1041; *adj.* bright, brilliant 579, 686, 1016 *etc.*; clear (*of water*) 644, 753, 799, 1041, (*of voice*) 1037, (*of sight*) 481; *adv.* clearly (*of voice*) 1057, (*of sight*) 1063; bright, light (*of day*) 1485; *sm.* light 498, 1130, 1758

cliner; *v.n.* bow 369, 659

clot, *ind.pr.3 of* **clore**, *v.a.* surround 1700

ço 9, 21, 85 *etc.*, **iço** 71, 102, 111 *etc.*, **içoe** 1794, **c'** 544; *demonstr. pron.neut.* this, that, it 85, 87, 93 *etc.*; all this 1084*n*; **pur ço** for that, this reason 299, 473, 533; **parmi tut ço** even so 462*n*; **si ço nun** if (you do) not, otherwise 1040; (i) **ço que, que ... ço,** *rel.pron.* what 9, 102, 127 *etc.*; **iço dunt** that for which 71; **de (i)ço que** *conj.* because, at the fact that 1440, 1820; **pur ço que** *conj.* because 21, 518; **sanz ço que** *conj.* without (the need that) 746; **devant içoe que** *conj.* before, until 1794; *cf.* **ja, nun², parmi**

cois (= **chois**), *sm.*: **prendre en sun c.** choose 1542

col, *sm.* neck 1017, 1571

cols, *nom.sg.* 510; *obl.pl.* **colps** 937, 1021; *sm.* blow 937, 1021; stroke (*of bell*) 510*n*

colur, *s.* colour 1694

comander *see* **cumander**

commo(u)t *see* **commoveir**

commoveir; *ind.pr.3* **commout** 1047; *pret.3* **commot** 1254; *v.a.* disturb 1047; move, stir 1254

comunalment, *adv.* together, all 113

concreit, *ind.pr.3 of* **concreire**, *v.a.* entrust 149

confés, *adj.*: **sei rendre c.** make confession 74, 337, 1299
conforter 1800, *v.a.* comfort, console
conseil *see* cunseil
conseller, *sm.* counsellor 502
contrarie, *s.* affliction 1390
converser, *v.n.* live 718
corde, *s.* rope 232, 385, 488, 1416
coroner; *v.a.* crown 1288
cors,[1] *sm.* body 217, 351, 739 *etc.*; physical needs 640, 1584; **mun c.** myself 1510*n*
cors,[2] *sm.* chorus 578
cose 503 *see* chose
coste, *s.*; **en c.** at (their) side 1660
costéd, *sm.* side 1292
costëer; *v.a.* go along the side of 1059
costil, *sm.* coast 430
crëablement, *adv.* with any confidence 1216
crëances, *s.pl.* beliefs 1052
creature, *s.* creation, creature 513
creint *see* cremer
creire 148; *ind.pr.1* crei 171, *3* creit 53, 105, 792, *5* creés 1091, crëez 1200, *6* creient 964; *fut.5* crerrez 476; *v.a.* believe 53, 171, 1200; believe in 105, 792; entrust 148; trust 1091; *v.n.* trust 476; *v.refl.* reckon oneself 964
creistre; *ind.pr.3* creist 1176; *fut.3* creistrat 3; *pret.3* crut 623, 788; *v.n.* increase 788, 1176; grow stronger 3, 623
cremer 924: *ind.pr.3* creint 1708, *6* crement 624, 651, 910 *etc.*; *v.a.* fear 624, 651, 910 *etc.*; *v.n.* be afraid 1005
creos 257, cros 635, *sm.* hollow
crïer; *v.n.* cry out 342, 557; *v.a.* cry out to, implore 189, 1257; cry out for, beg 306, 1246*n*
cristal, *sm.* crystal 272, 1094, 1690
criz, *s.pl.* cries 1168
croc, *sm.* hook 1468
cros *see* creos
crüels, *adj.pl.* cruel-looking 1045; *s.pl.* cruel people 1286

cruz, *sf.* cross 675, 1293; sign of the cross 1119
cuilir 1296; *pret.3* cuilit 1545; *v.a.* accept
culpe *see* clamer
cum 12, 30, 40 *etc.*, cume 166, 314, 315 *etc.*; *adv.* (*interrog.*) how 128; (*of manner*) how 141, 314, 315 *etc.*; as befits 40, 42, 116 *etc.*; *compar. and modal conj.* as 30, 144, 446 *etc.*; esi cum as 12, si cum as, like 54, 166, 482, 537 *etc.*; as if 1530; si cum (+ *subj.*) as if 1214; si ...cum as...as 1118; cume si as if 1377; tant cum as many as 179, 180; as long as 237, 731, 1829; as much as 245, 303–4, 1312; tant... cum 1356, itant ... cum(e) 389, 490 as ... as; itel ... cum 560, 1622 such ... as; tels cum as if 938; cum plus ... mielz the more ... the better 475–6; cum melz 1171, cum plus 1172 as best; cum ... plus as much as 604; cum plus ... plus the further ... the more 1100; cum plus ... e plus the more ... the more 1153; *conj.* (*temporal*) while 665, 1015 *etc.*; when 228, 241, 309 *etc.*; *cf.* plus, tant
cumander, comander; *ind.pr.1* cumant 1258, comant 1473; *v.a.* command 151, 403, 830 *etc.*; ask 9, 1441; *v.refl.* commend oneself 572
cumandise, *s.* command 1556
cumant 372, 995; *nom.sg.* cumanz 12; *sm.* command 372, 995; bidding 12
cume *see* cum
cument, *adv.* how 148, 150, 336 *etc.*
cumfort, *s.* consolation 560
cumpaignuns, *obl.pl.* 642, 1519; *nom.pl.* cumpaignun 1493; *s.pl.* companions
cumpaine, *sf.* company 592
cumpainie, *sf.* company 694, 890
cumplie, *sf.* compline 569*n*
cumungement, *s.* communion 347
cunduire; *ind.pr.3* cunduit 781, 1357,

1805, *6* **cundüent** 637; *pret.3* **cun-duit** 1551*n*; *pp.f.* **cunduite** 1161; *v.a.* guide 637, 781, 1551; drive 1161, 1357; **en c.** lead away 1805

cunduit 923, 1490, 1626, 1637; *nom.sg.* **cunduz** 378; *sm.* protection, guidance 378, 923, 1490, 1637; escort 1626

cungét 401, 608, 1605, 1803, **cungé** 145, 780; *obl.pl.* **cungez** 860; *sm.* leave, permission 860: **prendre c.** 145, 589, 608 *etc.*, **prendre le c.** 780, take leave

cunquerre 626, *v.a.* reach

cunrëer *v.a.* prepare 400, 451

cunrei 301, 331, 365 *etc.*, **cunreid** 787, 1580, 1584; *nom.sg.* **cunreiz** 974, 1586, 1588; *sm.* provisions 301, 365, 434 *etc.*; equipment 331, 459

cunseil 6, 73, **conseil** 79, 105; *obl.pl.* **cunseilz** 41; *sm.* advice 79, 105; wisdom, wise counsel, judgement 41; **prendre c.** decide 73

cunte, *s.* count, reckoning 1494

cunter, *v.a.* calculate 605: credit, count 1546*n*

cuntre, *prep.* against 1400; towards 1716; **c. terre** on the ground 1723

cuntredit, *ind.pr.3 of* **cuntredire**, *v.a.* resist 435

cuntresailiz, *pp. of* **cuntresailir**, *v.n.* rise up against 973

cuntretenir, *v.a.* oppose 928

cunuistre; *ind.pr.3* **cunuit** 931; *pret.3* **cunut** 195, **cunuit** 971; *pp.* **cunuit** 337; *v.a.* recognise 195, 931; know about 337; know 971

curages, *sm.nom.sg.* courage 224

curante, *adj.f.* swift 178; *cf.* **curre**

cure, *s.*: **sanz c.** carefree 761; **prendre c. de** care (about), wish (to) 162; take care (of) 352; pay heed (to) 514; **aveir c. de** take care (to) 803

curre; *ind.pr.3* **curt** 847, 898, 1142, *4* **curum** 1218, *6* **curent** 379; *ind. impf.3* **cureit** 809; *pret.6* **cururent** 219; *pres. p.* **curant** 645, **currant** 654, *pl.* **curanz** 188; *pp.* **curut** 480, 897, **curud** 98; *v.n.* run 188, 645, 654, 1142; sail 98, 219, 379 *etc.*; flow, course 898; **c. sus** descend (upon) 809; *v.a.* run with 1749; *cf.* **curante**

curs, *sm.* course 234, 610, 1112 *etc.*; voyage 613, 790, 1097; **a c. entrin** without interruption 1639; **a dreit c.** on a straight course 1663; *see also* **prendre, tendre**

custe, *sm.* torment 1312, 1328; **sanz c.** easily 585; without problem 861

cuverte, *adj.f.* covered 1166

d' *see* **de**

dampnez, *pp.adj.nom.sg.m.* damned 1300; *sm.nom.pl.* the damned 1168, 1178

danz *see* **donz**

de 3, 13, 19 *etc.*, **d'** 119, 124, 254 *etc.*; (*with article*) **del** 86, 140, 162 *etc.*, **des** 20, 100, 138 *etc.*; (*locative*) of, from 3, 25, 86 *etc.*; (*origin*) of 19, 20, 21 *etc.*; (*source*) from 37, 79, 80 *etc.*; (*movement*) from 119, 170, 191 *etc.*; (*possessive*) of 24, 99, 364 *etc.*; (+ *pron.* = *poss.adj.*) 33, 124, 907; (*qualifying*) 29, 40, 41 *etc.*; (*partitive*) 184, 312, 449 *etc.*; (*partitive after numeral*) of 107, 156, 199 *etc.*; (*partitive after expression of quantity*) of 290, 331, 379 *etc.*; (*respective*) about, concerning 13, 147, 365 *etc.*; for 141, as regards 493*n*; (*comparative*) than 704, 845; (*instrumental*) : (*material*) with, of 175, 176, 272 *etc.*; (*agent*) by, from 253, 289, 499 *etc.*; (*cause*) from 422, 1588; (*verb* + **de** + *inf.*) 43, 135, 162 *etc.*; (*verb* + **de** + *noun or pron.*) 47, 52, 118 *etc.*; *cf.also* **ço, fors, haltece, ici, lu, luin, mielz, poi, pres, tant**

debarder; *v.a.* squander 1272

debuter; *v.a.* cast aside 1052

decés, *s.*: **prendre d.** die 736

declinant, *sm.* end (*of day*) 555
dedenz, *adv.* on the inside 175; *prep.* inside 271
deduit, *s.* joy, happiness 1625, 1638
defaile, *s.* loss of strength 238
defalte, *s.* lack (*of provisions*) 602: **sanz d.** without interruption 248, 1639
defendre; *ind.pr.1* **defent** 296, 647; *pret.1* **defendi** 1279; *imper.2* **defent** 14; *v.a.* protect 14; forbid 296, 647; deny 1279*n*
defens, *sm.* protection 1006*n*
defire 1386, *v.n.* perish
defors, *adv.* on the outside 176, 1402
dehait, *s.* sorrow 154
dehaite, *s.* affliction 1761
dehaitez, *adj.nom.sg.m.* wretched 1290
deiable *see* **diable**
deient, deies *see* **deveir**
deintez, *s.pl.* delicacies 702
dejus, *adv.* below 1234
dejuste, *adv.* close by 1327
del *see* **de**
delacherez, *pp.adj.* lacerated 1224
delicïus, *adj.* delightful 1737*n*
delit, *sm.* delight 24, 1594, 1774
demain, *adv.* tomorrow 426, 427; *sm.* next day 963
demaine *see* **demener**
demander 26, *v.a.* ask 26, 1444
demener; *ind.pr.1* **demaine** 1302, *2* **demeines** 1319; *v.a.* undergo 1302; *v.refl.* exist, live 1319
demurance, *s.* delay 122
demurer 1603; *ind.pr.1* **demoir** 1348, *4* **demurum** 1217; *fut.1* **demurai** 863; *pret.3* **demurat** 926, 1183; *v.n.* be late, fail to appear 863; be long in coming 926; delay 1217, 1603; remain 1348; *v.n.* (*impers.*) be a delay 1183*n*
deners, *s.pl.* money 1295
denz,[1] *sm.pl.* teeth 913, 939, 942, 949
denz,[2] *adv.* in it 799
departir 892; *ind.pr.3* **depart** 1155, 1340, 1341; *v.n.* split up 1155; *v.a.* separate 1340, 1341; *sm.* departure 892

deport, *ind.pr.1 of* **deporter,** *v.a.* be spared 1308
dereine, *adj.f.* last to come, latter 947
derube, *sm.* cliff 170
des[1] *see* **de**
des,[2] *prep.* from 495, 767, 1072; **d. quant** how long 715
descendre; *ind.pr.1* **descent** 1349, **descen** 1416, *3* **descent** 1007, 1072, 1080 *etc.*; *ind.impf.3* **descendeit** 1070; *pret.3* **descendit** 172; *v.n.* go down, descend 172, 1072, 1080, 1349, 1416; come down 1007; slope 1191*n*
descirer; *v.a.* tear 950, 1224
descorder; *v.a.* create division, discord 1270
descuverz, *pp.nom.sg.m. of* **descuvrir,** v.a. uncover 1205
desdeign 236, **desdein** 530; *s.*; **par nul d.** without resentment? 236*n*; **prendre en d.** disdain 530
deseriter; *v.a.* disinherit 52, 533
desesperer 953, *v.n.* despair
desir, *s.* what (one) desires 1102; desire 71; *see* **prendre**
desirer; *v.a.* wish 217, 288
desplout, *pret.3 of* **desplaisir,** *v.n.* displease 277
desque[1] 192, 220, 495 *etc.*, **desqu'** 367, 1069, 1806, *conj.* until 220, 367, 822 *etc.*; *prep.* until 769, 862; **d. a** until 831, 841, 1087 *etc.*; up to 192, 936, 1069, 1209; **d. en** as far as 708; into 1806; down to 495, 1043; **d. ci** as far as here 192; **desque la que** until 1614
desque[2] 347, **desqu'** 815, *conj.* as soon as
desrei, *sm.* excess 302
destiner; *v.a.* destine 796, 798, 1832
destre, *sf.* right hand 207, 661; **a d.** on the right 1235
destrecce, *s.* force 1186
desur, *prep.* on 511, 611, 1697

desus, *adv.* above 1233; over it 1458; on top (of it) 1699

desuz, *adv.* below 257

detenuz, *pp. of* **detenir,** *v.a.* hold prisoner 1496

detirer; *v.a.* tear at 949; *pp.* **detirez** battered 1223

detriers, *adv.* behind 1232, 1234

devaler; *v.n.* fly down 554

devant, *adv.* (*place*) before, in front 634, 1233, 1453; (*time*) before, previously 836, 856; *prep.* (*place*) before 341, 542, 699; (*time*) ahead of, earlier than 478*n*; before 392; within 994; **d. içoe que** until 1794

deveir; *ind.pr.3* **deit** 150, 243, 504 *etc.,* *4* **devum** 755, *6* **deient** 232, 670, 1614; *fut.6* **devrunt** 62, 63, 234; *condit.3* **devreit** 56; *pret.1* **dui** 1270, *3* **dout** 158, **dut** 526, *6* **dourent** 610; *subj.pr.2* **deies** 516; *subj. impf.3* **doust** 1702; *v.n.* must, be obliged to 56, 150, 243 *etc.*; be (destined) to 62, 63, 232 *etc.*; have the duty of 526; be supposed to 755; mean 504*n*, 1442; have as purpose 516

devenir; *pret.3* **devint** 91; *pp.* **devenuz** 1495; *v.n.* end up 91; become 1495

devoler; *v.n.* fly down 882; *v.pron.* fly down 508

di 392, 400, 749 *etc.,* *pl.* **dis** 183, 404, 591 *etc.*; day 392, 590, 749 *etc.*; **di pascal** 400, **di paschur** 843 Easter Day; **tuz dis** always 591, 1554, 1567 *etc.*; **tot dis, tot di** constantly 1358; **de di en di** for ever 1300

dïable 314, 342, 1324, 1364, **deiable** 1431, 1465, 1479; *sm.* devil, demon

dïemaine *see* **dimaine**

digne, *adj.* worthy, excellent 664

dimaine 1305, **dïemaine** 1315, *s.* Sunday

dire; *ind.pr.1* **di** 117, 515, 1255 *etc.*; *3* **dit** 15, 23, 54 *etc.,* *6* **dïent** 576, 1038, 1471; *pret.3* **dist** 185, 295, 329 *etc.*; *subj.pr.2* **dïes** 1258, *3* **dïet** 1441; *pp.* **dist** 147, 198, 203 *etc.,* **dit** 109, 1197, 1527; say 185, 295, 329 *etc.*; tell 15, 23, 54, 109 *etc.*; recite 576

dis¹, *num.adj.* ten 465, 1146, 1377, 1407

dis² *see* **di**

divers, *adj.pl.* various 35

divin 477, 918, 1643; *f.* **divine** 2; *adj.* divine 2, 477, 1643; *sm.* holy man 918

diviser; *v.a.* describe in detail 1773*n*

divisïuns, *s.pl.* explanations 1778

diz, *s.pl.* sayings 81; what one has to say 124; words 514, 651, 806

doile, *subj. pr.3 of* **doleir,** *v.pron.* suffer 18

dolent 1467; *nom.sg.* **dolenz** 1255; *sm.* wretch

dolur, *sm.* sorrow 1250; pain, torment 1426, 1440, 1538

donna, *sf.* lady (*title of address*) 1

donz 194, 454, **danz** 8, *sm.* master (*title of address*) 194, 454; **dom** 8

dormir 320; *ind.pr.6* **dorment** 573; *pres.p.* **dormant** 810; *pres.p.adj.f.* **dormante** 895; *v.n.* sleep 320, 573, 810; *pres.p.adj.* still 895

doul, *sm.* wretchedness, grief 1268

dourent *see* **deveir**

dous 199, 588, 591 *etc.*; *nom.* **dui** 112, 1329, **dous** 933; *num.adj.* two; **dui e dui** in pairs 112

dou(s)t *see* **deveir**

douz *see* **dulz**

draguns, *nom.sg.* 1016, 1023, 1027; *pl.* 1705, 1722; *sm.* dragon, monster

drap 1225, 1450; *nom.sg.* **dras** 1442; *pl.* **dras** 29, 462, 828; *sm.sg.* cloth 1225, 1442, 1450; *pl.* habit, clothing 29, 462, 828

drecher; *v.a.* raise 204, 209, 658, 934; direct 383, 1018

dreit 56, 1610, 1720 *etc.*; *nom.sg.* **dreiz** 18, 1810; *s.* **par d.** by right 56; *adj.* right 18; straight 1610; correct 1720; rightful 1810; *adv.*

straight 267, 1148, 1467; right (at) 1707; **tut d.** straight 1623, 1703; straight down 170; **d. cum** just when 929

duble, *adj.* double 643; increased 1482

dubler; *v.a.* increase, augment 765*n*

dui *see* **dous, deveir**

duit¹, *ind.pr.3 of* **duire**; *v.a.* lead 266, 692

duit² 487, 489, 799; *nom.sg.* **duiz** 636; *nom.pl.* **duit** 650; *obl.pl.* **duiz** 751; *sm.* stream

dulcement, *adv.* sweetly 509; gently 1721

dulceur, *s.* friendliness 689

dulz 146, 668, 699 *etc.*, **douz** 395; *f.sg.* **dulce** 704, 997; *f.pl.* **dulces** 557; *adj.* kind 146, 1820; good 395; cheerful 668; sweet (*of taste*) 699; dear 1292

dum *see* **dun²**

dun¹, *sm.* gift 582

dun² 52, 276, 286 *etc.*, **dunt** 48, 71, 174 *etc.*, **dum** 810, 882, 1442 *etc.*; *rel.pron.* about which 48; from which 52, 554, 752 *etc.*; with which 174, 276, 450 *etc.*; of which 71, 286, 1646; by which 1566, 1602; because of which 810; of whom 1132 (*absolute*) that with which 397*n*; (*interrog.adv.*) from where 1444

dunc 112, 123, 135 *etc.*, **dunches** 769; *adv.* then (*time*) 112, 123, 135 *etc.*; then (*consequence*) 514; *cf.* **idunc**

duner; *fut.3* **durat** 362; *v.a.* give 362, 978, 1691; grant 1605; *v.refl.* exchange 937

dunt *see* **dun**

dur 272, 1695; *nom.sg.* **durs** 1383; *f.* **dure** 762; *adj.* hard, solid 272, 1383, 1695; difficult 762

durat *see* **duner**

durement, *adv.* exceedingly 165

durer; *v.n.* last 161, 237

dut *see* **deveir**

dutance, *s.* **entrer en d.** become afraid 919

dute, *sf.* fear 1501

duter; *v.n.* be afraid 485; (**de**) be afraid (of) 1051; *v.a.* fear 863, 991, 1181

e, *conj.* (*introducing clause*) and 4, 15, 17 *etc.*; (*joining phrases or words*) and 7, 11, 41 *etc.*; **e ... e** both ... and 31, 45, 58 *etc.*; *cf.* **si¹**

eals *see* **il**

eglise, *s.* church 446

egre *see* **aigre**

eigue *see* **aigue**

eir, *sm.* heir 27, 1648*n*

eire, *sm.* voyage 141, 147, 244 *etc.*

eirent *see* **errer**

eisi 1015, 1177, 1641, **eissi** 439, 593, **esi** 12, **issi** 1249, *adv.* in such a way 439; in this way 1015, 1249, 1641; so 1177; **esi cum** as 12; **cum ... eissi** as ... so 593; *cf.* **cum**

eisil, *s.* exile 30, 559

eisir 484, *ind.pr.4* **eisums** 639, **eisum** 834; *ind.pr.6* **eisent** 265, 641, **eissent** 441, **issent** 1665; *fut.1* **istrai** 1509; *pret.3* **eisit** 342, 1134, 1515, 6 **issirent** 1000; *pp.* **eisud** 688, **eisut** 1667; *v.n.* come out 342, 1134, 1515, 1665; **fors e.** go out 688; disembark 639, 834; *v.pron.* **s'en e.** disembark 265, 441, 641; depart 1000; emerge 1667; **fors s'en e.** disembark 1509; *subst.inf.* landing 484

eissi *see* **eisi**

eissil = **eissi** + **le** 593*n*

el¹ = **en** + **le**; *see* **en¹**

el², *indef.pron.* something else 903, 1825; anything else 1376; **tut el** everything else 959; (+ *neg.*) nothing else 741; *see also* **un**

eles, *sf.pl.* wings 1017

els *see* **il**

em *see* **en²**

emblét, *s.*: **an e.** by stealth 311

empeintes, *s.pl.* assaults, attacks 1237

emperur, *s.* emperor 270
emprent *see* enprendre
en[1] 6, 11, 77 *etc.*, an 311; (*with article*)
el 355, 1359, 1365 *etc.*, es 1145,
1320, 1575; *prep.* (*locative*) in 6,
77, 96 *etc.*; into 11, 125, 255 *etc.*;
on 83, 93, 320 *etc.*; out to 90, 783;
at 785 (*with* mer); under 594; to
815; within 1089; en + *gerund*
1154; enz en, *see* enz[2]; *see also*
desque[1]; (*temporal*) in, during 30,
559, 836 *etc.*; at 579; within 1813;
see di; (*in adverbial locutions*) *see*
aines 1711, brande 900, cois 1542,
coste 1660, desdein 530, dutance
919, emblét 311, fei 116, jus 1348,
larecin 1272, lu 701, luin 256,
munt 1339, primers 1669, repos(t)
318, 350, 1558, sus 1069, tresturn
1354, val 1339, 1389; *see also* di
en[2] 25 *etc.*, an 770, em 800, 805, 807
etc., ent 295, 941; *pron.* (*respective*) about it 59, 73, 112 *etc.*;
because of it, this 105, 120, 196
etc.; of it 369; for it 1026, 1028;
(*partitive, usually after expressions
of quantity*) of it 25, 180, 245 *etc.*;
some 295; *adv.* (*with verbs of
motion*) away, from there, out: *cf.*
aler 349, 432, 449 *etc.*, s'en aler
157, 210, 370 *etc.*, cunduire 1805,
s'en devoler 508, s'en eisir 265,
441, 641 *etc.*, s'en fuïr 464, s'en
lever 705, mener 115, 119, 130
etc., porter 1012, 1601, 1799, s'en
raler 860, sailir 941, 1196, turner
427, s'en turner 328, 832, 1486,
s'en venir 1540
enartét, *adj.* skilled 1692
enbraise, *ind.pr.3 of* enbraser, *v.n.*
burn bright 907
encassét, *pp.pl.* set 680*n*
encensers, *sm.pl.* censers 679
enchaced, *ind.pr.3 of* enchacer, *v.a.*
pursue 906
enchäer 657, *v.n.* fall down
enclins, *adj.nom.sg.m.* prostrate 811
enclose, *pp.adj.f.* surrounded 1107

encröez, *pp.adj.nom.sg.m.* hooked
on, hung up 1355
encui, *adv.* today 340
endemain, *s.* next day 1621
endormit, *pp.adj.pl.* asleep 309
endreit[1], *prep.* near 1131
endreit[2], *s.* place 1319
endurer; *v.a.* endure 1171
enemis, *s.nom.sg.* enemy 988
eneveis, *adv.* soon 1430*n*
enfermetét, *s.* sickness 739; *cf.* enfertét
enfern 65, 1116, 1120 *etc.*; *nom.sg.*
enfers 1207; *nom.pl.* enfern 1329;
obl.pl. enfers 1327, 1341; *sm.* Hell
enfertét, *s.* sickness 422; *cf.* enfermetét
enfler; *v.n.* swell up 1423
enforcer 1380; *v.a.* increase
engemmét, *pp.adj.pl.* studded 676
enhorter; *v.a.* exhort 1274
enlüez, *pp.nom.sg.m. of* enlüer, *v.a.*
smear 1382
enmaler; *v.a.* secrete, stow away 318
ennois, *sm.pl.* trials, suffering 614
ennuiot *see* annuier
enposte, *adj. f.* dark 1608
enprendre; *ind.pr.3* enprent 106,
244, 660, 1153, emprent 759;
pret.3 enprist 114; *pp.* enpris 9; *v.a.*
undertake 9, 106, 114, 244; *v.n.*
light, catch fire 759, 1153; (+ *inf.*)
begin 660
enruit, *ind.pr.3 of* enruire, *v.n.* roar
1125
ensaintir; *v.n.* lead saintly life 1827
ensample, *sm.* example 37; exemplary story 82
enseignes, *s.pl.* tokens 1800, 1802
enseigner; *subj.pr.3* enseint 129; *v.a.*
instruct 129, 1114; explain 714;
show the way 1526
ensemble, *adv.*: e. od together with
577, 782
ensemblét, *pp.* collected 312
enserrét, *pp.adj.nom.pl.m.* perplexed
1498; in distress 1822
ent *see* en[2]

entailét, *pp.adj.nom.pl.m.* decorated 276*n*

enteins, *adv.*: n'e. not even 332

entendre 1784; *ind.pr.3* entent 22, 160; *v.a.* understand 1784; *v.n.* (+ a) be intent upon 22; (+ *inf.*) intend 160

enter, *adj.* whole 327, 615, 678, 748; sound, seaworthy 600

entre, *prep.* between 748, 1374, 1428; among 70

entrebat, *s.* interruption 1314*n*

entreduner; *v.refl.* give each other, exchange 1022

entree 630, 797, 1704, 1727, entrethe 251, *sf.* landing place 251, 630, 797; entrance 1704, 1727

entremis, *pp. of* entremetre, *v.a.* undertake 10*n*

entreporter; *v.refl.* reflect 1693

entrer 158, 193, 616 *etc.*, *v.n.* enter 92, 271, 280 *etc.*; set out, embark 158; (*usually with* en nef) board 185, 424, 463 *etc.*; e. en mer put out to sea 783, 1633; e. a enter the service of 193*n*; *v.a.* e. païs touch land 616*n*; *subst.inf.* entrance 1707; *see also* dutance

entrin, *adj.* sincere 443; perfect 684; whole 812; in one piece 1677; *see also* curs

enturn, *adv.* around 1059, 1071; ici e. here 588

enveier; *v.a.* send 139, 562

enz[1] 427, 1004 *see* ainz

enz[2], *adv.* on board 184, 442, 792, 1637; in it 680, 1398; on it 1355; enz en in 131, 142, 558 *etc.*; inside 281; on board 463; up in 520; into 1657; enz a on, in 571; en enz on board 185*n*; inside 280

eols *see* il

er, *adv.* yesterday 1427

erbe 1741; *pl.* herbes 802, *s.* grass 1741; herbs 802

erbeie, *s.* grassland, meadow 967

ere *see* estre[1]

ermite *see* hermite

errer 194, 595, 894; *ind.pr.6* eirent 372; *ind.impf.3* errout 322; *pp.* errét 1497, 1821; *v.n.* travel, journey 194, 894; fare 1497, 1821; *subst.inf.* journey, departure 595

ert *see* estre[1]

es = en + les; *see* en[1]

escalféd 909; *nom.sg.m.* eschalfez 1134; *adj.* burning hot

eschele, *sf.* bell 510, 711

eschipede, *pp.f. of* eschiper, *v.n.* moor 252*n*

eschiver; *v.n.* escape 1172; *v.pron.* (+ de) avoid 484*n*

escive, *adj.f.* forbidding, hostile 1508

esclair, *s.* lightning 1020

escorcer; *v.a.* flay 1401, 1407

escordement, *adv.* fervently 205

escrïer; *v.a.* revile 1364; *v.pron.* shout 453

escripture, *s.* scripture 23

escrit, *s.* scripture 830

escuil, *s.*: prendre e. presume, jump at the opportunity (to) 68

esculante, *adj.f.* swift sailing 177

escuz, *s.pl.* shields 938

esforcer; *v.pron.* struggle, strive 1111

esgoier; *v.pron.* rejoice 1780

esguarder; *v.a.* survey 279

esguarer 1636, *subst.inf.* losing one's way

esi 12 *see* eisi

eslever; *v.pron.* (+ vers) rise up (against) 524

eslire; *ind.pr.3* eslist 107; *pp.* esliz 32, 123; *v.a.* choose

esmaier; *imper.5* esmaëz 365; *v.n.* be dismayed, concerned 365; *v.pron.* be dismayed, afraid 221, 226, 903, 973

esmaragde, *s.* emerald 1079, 1686

espace, *s.* space, width 1656; en grant e. for a long while 990

espandre; *ind.pr.3* espant 1170, 6 espandent 571; *subj.pr.3* espande 1420; *v.n.* burst 1420; *v.refl.* lie down 571; spread 1170

espëer; *v.a.* put on a spit 1367

espeines,*s.pl.* acts of expiation 1321*n*

espeir, *s.*: **a lur e.** as they had hoped 381

espeirer; *v.a.* expect 1220

espesse, *adj.f.* thick 791

espiez, *s.pl.* spears 940

espines, *s.pl.* thorns 1288

espirit, *sm.* soul 349, 1560; spirit, power 1030; *cf.* **Saint Espirit**

espleiter, *v.n.* fare 1182

estage, *sm.* height 1188

estait *see* **ester**

estals, *s.pl.* stalls (*in church*) 708

esteint, *ind.pr.3 of* esteindre, *v.n.* go out (*of lamp*) 759

esteit *see* **ester**, **estre**

estelét *adj.* starry 1278

estenceles, *s.pl.* sparks 1127

estent, *ind.pr.3 of* estendre, *v.refl.* extend 165, 497, 1192

esteot *see* **estuveir**

ester 1505; *ind.pr3* estait 1477, 1769, esteit 1699*n*, 6 estunt 404, 839, 1087 *etc.*; *ind.impf.3* estout 77; *v.n.* stay, remain 404, 839, 1087 *etc.*; stand 1505, 1699; live 77

estét, *s.* summer 1240, 1330, 1554, 1745

estorce 1476, estorse 958, *s.* rescue, escape 958*n*; **a l'e.** in the end 1476*n*

estorie, *s.*: **veir' e.** scripture 54

estot *see* **estuveir**

estout *see* **ester**, **estuveir**

estre¹ 29, 118, 600 *etc.*; *ind.pr.1* sui 1199, 1267, 1269 *etc.*, *2* es 513, 1243, 1259 *etc.*, *3* est 18, 51, 71 *etc.*, *4* sumes 191, 519, 533 *etc.*, *5* estes 1116, 1788, 6 sunt 250, 255, 261 *etc.*; *fut.3* ert 201, 864, 1244, estrat 1759, *5* estrez 588, streiz 859; *condit.3* estreit 615, 1068, 6 estreient 618; *ind.impf.3* ert 6, 38, 40 *etc.*, ere 86, 222, 442, 988, esteit 98, 1293, 1675, 6 erent 249, 389, 560 *etc.*; *pret.1* fui 1290, 1541, 1576 *etc.*, *3* fud 21, 32, 50 *etc.*, fut 525, 1215, fu 527, *4* fumes 52, 520,

6 furent 309, 808, 848, 1822; *subj.pr.1* seie 1244, 1394, 2 seies 515, *3* seit 14, 122, 503 *etc.*, seient 632; *subj.impf.3* fust 88, 178, 252 *etc.*; *imper.5* sëez 359; *pp.* estét 1539, 1553; *v.n.* be 6, 12, 14 *etc.*; *v.n. (impers.)* be 1177; *v.aux.* (*usually with verbs of motion*) 19, 98, 191 *etc.*; (+ *gerund*) 540, 1105, 1518*n*; *subst.inf.* nature 413

estre², *s.* dwelling-place 662, 1526

estreits, *adj.nom.sg.m.* narrow 169

estulte, *adj.f.* fierce 945

estunt *see* **ester**

esturbeiluns, *sm.nom.sg.* whirlwind 1149

esturdïer; *v.a.* make dizzy 1712

estuveir; *ind.pr.3* estout 246, 587, 1048, 1112, esteot 16, estot 1631; *ind.impf.3* estuveit 916; *pret.3* estout 179, 304, 326, 528; *v.impers.* be necessary, must

ethez, *sm.nom.sg.* age 1592

ewage, *s.* channel 567

fai *see* **fei**, **faire**

faile, *s.*: **faire f.** run out, run low 367

failir; *ind.pr.3* falt 411, 901; *fut.3* faldrat 1240; *subj.pr.3* failet 994, 1520, 6 failent 787, 1494; *pp.* falit 222, *nom.sg.* failiz 974; *v.n.* drop (*of wind*) 222; be lacking 411; run low 974, 994; fail to take place 1240*n*; be absent 1520; (+ **a**) lack 787, 1494; *see also* **poi**

faim, *s.* hunger 788, 819, 1174 *etc.*

faire 136, 174, 245 *etc.*; *ind.pr.1* faz 1474, *3* fait 15, 138, 346 *etc.*, *6* funt 275, 450, 556 *etc.*; *fut.2* fras 426, 1040, 1597, *3* frat 367, 1560, 1627, ferat 920*n*, *5* frez 551, freiz 874, 877, 879; *condit.3* fereit 43; *pret.1* fis 1269, 1446, 1457, *3* fist 173, 174, 177 *etc.*, *4* feïmes 470, *6* firent 351, 444, 466 *etc.*; *imper.2* fai 1434, 1436, 1799, *4* faimes 132; *pp.* fait 319, 445, 531 *etc.*, *f.* faite 274; *v.a.* do 15, 136, 403 *etc.*; make

450, 466, 636 *etc.*; build 174, 272, 274 *etc.*; create 1278, 1385; celebrate 397, 426, 444, *etc.*; cover, travel 613, 1097; commit 319; sing 556; wreak 951; (*repeating sense of a previous verb*) 510, 1356; (*causal + inf.*) 173, 174, 673 *etc.*; (*in locutions with subst. or indef. pron.*) *cf.* aise 986, clartét 275, faile 367, fin 43, 842, 853, merci 338, nïent 1636, peis 1582*n*, processïun 690, raëncune 421, respuns 667, return 1597, seignacle 1807, seivrement 1560, semblant 1269, tresturn 138; *v.refl.* act as 1717; *subst.inf.* construction 1678

fais, *s.* burden, load 1146

fait *see* fei, faire

faitiz, *pp.adj.nom.sg.* neatly set 264

faitres, *sm.nom.sg.* maker 1676

faidrat, falt, falit *see* failir

fals, *adj.* false 28

faz *see* faire

féd, *sm.* fellow 1450; demon 1132*n*; *cf.* malféd

fedeil 580; *nom.sg.* fedeilz 77; *nom.pl.* fetheil 210; *obl.pl.* fetheilz 206, 242; *sm.* faithful follower

fei 116, feid 806, 1673, fai 70, 298, fait 954, *sf.* faith 70, 116, 298 *etc.*; en f. veire for sure 1673; tenir f. a obey 806

feignent, *ind.pr.6 of* feindre, *v.pron.* be slack, idle 215, 1099

feïmes *see* faire

feiz, *s.pl.* times 7, 591, 1407

fels, *nom.sg.* 529, 1281; *nom.pl.* felun 67; *sm.* traitor 67, 1281; *adj.* treacherous 529

fent, *ind.pr.1 of* fendre, *v.n.* burst 1424

fer, *s.* iron 1135, 1375, 1713

ferir; *ind.pr.3* fert 1231, 6 ferent 1229; *v.a.* strike, batter

ferliez, *pp.nom.sg. of* ferlïer, *v.a.* bind, chain 1363

fermement, *adv.* firmly 734

fermer; *v.a.* tie up 265, 865; fix, set 1083; place firmly 1179

fertres, *s.pl.* reliquaries, caskets 675

festal, *adj.*: a di f. on a feast day 749

feste, *sf.* (religious) feast 397, 426, 470 *etc.*

festïer 842, *v.n.* celebrate

festival, *adj.* magnificent 1093

fetheil *see* fedeil

feu *see* fiu

fi, *adj.* certain 118

fiance, *s.* trust 1179

fichét, *pp.* fixed 1375

fier; *v.pron.* (+ en) put one's trust (in) 1659

filiol, *sm.* godson 84

filz, *sm.* son 116; *see also* Filz Deu, Filz Marie

fin¹, *sf.* end 628, 1230, 1350; purpose 22; sanz f. continually 1755; aveir f. come to an end 1230; faire f. cease 43, 842, 853; prendre sa f. die 719*n*; saveir f. see an end to 1098

fin², *adj.* pure 1084, 1698

finer; *v.n.* die 1831

fiu 721, feu 270; *nom.sg.* fius 1324, 1810, *sm.* fief, estate

flairer; *v.n.* smell 1735

flaistre, *adj.* putrid 1105

flamme, *sf.* flame 909, 1021, 1128 *etc.*

flammer; *pres.p.adj.nom.sg.m.* flammanz 1007, 1016, *pl.* 1138; *f.pl.* flammantes 1009; *v.n.* blaze 1683; *adj.* flaming 1007, 1009, 1016, 1138

floter; *v.n.* float 883

flum, *s.pl.* rivers 1748, 1749

flur, *sm.* flower 96, 1700, 1735 *etc.*

flurie, *adj.f.* full of flowers 1734

fol, *nom.pl.m.* 808; *obl.pl.m.* fols 816, 1050, *f.* fole 921, 1414; *adj.* foolish 808, 816, 921, 1050; terrible 1414; *cf.* fols

folie, *s.* foolish things 1446

fols 1378, fous 1125, *s.pl.* bellows

force, *s*. strength 239, 1154; **par f.** 32, **a f.** 1475 by compulsion

forcer, *v.a.* force 1408

forfaire; *pret.1* forfis 1247, *3* forfist 57; *v.n.* do wrong 57; commit a crime 1247

forfait, *sm.* crime 1260

forge, *sf.* forge 1142

forment, *adv.* very 42, 292, 684 *etc.*; greatly 333, 1688

fornaise, *s*. furnace 908

fors, *adv.* out, outside: *cf.* aler 218, eissir 639, 834, s'en eissir 441, 1509, sailir 963, en sailir 1196; metre f. expel 58; estre f. be out of torment 1244*n*; de f. from outside 1583; *prep.* except 214, 263, 698 *etc.*; f. sul except 92, 442, 1510; f. sul (+ *neg.*) only 283, 539, 913; ne ...f. only 155–6, 1183, 1641–2; f. de out of 344, 673

fort 258, 626, 668 *etc.*; *nom.sg.* forz 1024; *obl.pl.* forz 957; *f.* forte 896, 1704; *adj.* grave 258, 957; strong 1011, 1024, 1458; severe 1398; (+ a + *inf.*) difficult (to) 626, 896; *adv.* warmly 668; greatly, very much 909, 1423; strongly, fiercely 949, 1394; very, extremely 1010; firmly 1227; violently 1229

fosses, *s.pl.* pits 1123

fous[1] 1125 *see* fols

fou(s)[2] *see* fu

fras, frat *see* faire

freid 1391, 1393, 1396; *nom.sg.* freiz 753, 1346; *obl.pl.* freiz 1174, 1425, 1761; *adj.* cold 753, 1346; *sm.* cold 1174, 1396, 1425, 1761; aveir f. be cold 1393

freidur, *s*. chill 898

fre(i)z *see* faire

frere 221, 236, 345 *etc.*, frerre 85, *sm.* monk 85, 221, 236 *etc.*; (*address*) brother 467, 987, 1593

fruit 1738; *nom.sg.* fruiz 1746; *sm.* fruit

fu 1394, fou 466, 756; *nom.sg.* fus 907, 1020, 1138 *etc.*, fous 757, 935; *obl.pl.* fus 1207, 1374, 1378; *sm.* fire

fuiles, *sf.pl.* leaves 491

fuïr; *ind.pr.3* fuit 24, 464; *impf.subj.6* fuïssent 914; *imper.4* fuium 817; *v.a.* flee 24, 817, 914; *v.pron.* s'en f. move away 464

fuisun 387, fusun 1740, *s*. abundance

fuite, *s*.: prendre f. flee 1162

fuler; *v.a.* push down, trample 1404

fum, *sm.* smoke 1105, 1205

fumante, *pres.p.adj.f.* smoking 1105

fumé, *sm.* smoke 1166*n*, 1170*n*

funde, *s*. sling 1152

fundre; *ind.pr.3* funt 1231, *6* fundent 892; *v.a.* shed 892; *v.n.* collapse, perish 1231

funs, *s.pl.* bottom, bed 1070

funt *see* fundre, faire

funtaine, *sf.* spring 643, 997, 1585

fus *see* fu

fust 175; *obl.pl.* fuz 461; *s*. wood 175; poles 461

fusun *see* fuisun

gabéth, *pp. of* gaber, *v.a.* mock 14

gabs, *s.pl.obl.* taunts 1287

gaiole, *s*. prison 1413

galeste, *sf.* stone, slingshot 1152

galiz, *pp.nom.sg. of* galir, *v.a.* hurl 1359

gals, *sm.*: a chant de g. at cockrow 575

gardins, *s.nom.sg.* garden 1733

gemmes, *s.pl.* precious stones 275, 680, 1679

gent, *sf.* people, inhabitants 648; humaine g. human beings 561

gesir 1723; *ind.pr.1* gis 1417; *ind. impf.3* giseit 811, *6* giseient 810; *subj.impf.3* goüst 1378; *v.n.* lie

gettent, gettes *see* jeter

gis, gisei(en)t *see* gesir

glaive 1725; *nom.sg.* glavies 1707; *sm.* sword

glorie, *sf.* heavenly glory 53, 541, 1728 *etc.*; praise 1028, 1033; heavenly reward 1548

goës, *s.pl.* jaws 1009

goie, *sf.* joy 689, 1638, 1767
goïr; *pret.3* goït 668, 6 goïrent 852; *pres.p.* goïsant 1060; *pp.* goïd 564, goït 1110; *v.a.* welcome 564, 668, 852, 1110; rejoice in 1060
gorge, *sf.* mouth 1141
gort, *sm.* stream 168, 855
goüst *see* gesir
grace, *sf.* grace 230, 989; *pl.* thanks 1606
gracïer; *v.a.* thank 186, 565, 622
graindre *see* greignur
grant 40, 154, 350 *etc.*; *nom.sg.m.* granz 241, 1023, 1133 *etc.*, grant 268; *nom.pl.m.* grant 633; *obl.pl.m.* granz 41, 942, 1045 *etc.*, grant 410*n*, 609; *f.sg.* grande 240, 247, 290 *etc.*, grant 53, 157, 275 *etc.*; *f.pl.* grandes 389, 684, 1647, granz 1175, 1310; *adj.* great 40, 41, 53 *etc.*; large 157, 247, 418 *etc.*; tall 654
gref, *adj.* difficult 128
greignur 1580; *nom.sg.* graindre 1250, graindres 1004; *obl.pl.* greinurs 471; *adj. compar.* greater 1004, 1250, 1580; *adj. superl.*: les g. the biggest 471*n*
greine, *s.* snarl, hostility 1481
gripun 1018; *nom.sg.* grips 1007*n*, 1023, 1025; *sm.* griffin
grisolites, *s.pl.* chrysolites 1681*n*
grisopase, *s.* chrysoprase 1684*n*
grosses, *adj.f.pl.* huge 1124
gruign, *sm.* promontory 166, 167
guairs, *adv.*: ne . . . g. not much 1110; n'i ad g. not far away 1325
guarant 1118, 1454, 1474, 1488; *nom.sg.* guaranz 1054; *sm.* protector 1054, 1474; protection 1118, 1454, 1488
guarder 150; *ind.pr.1* guart 1420; *subj.pr.3* guart 890; *pp.f.* gwardee 837; *v.a.* take care of 150; protect 206, 890; keep 837, 1271, 1449; *v.n.* see to it, take care (that) 921; ne g. quant be constantly afraid that 1420*n*

guarir 1714; *ind.impf.6* guariseient 1460; *subj.pres.2* guarisses 1602; *v.n.* be saved 1460, 1602; provide protection 1714
guarisun, *sf.* provisions 181
guarnir 299; *v.a.* warn 299; equip 1632; *v.refl.* provide, equip o.s. 601, 996, 999
guarrere, *sf.* adversary 931
guasteus, *sm.obl.pl.* loaves 410
guerpir; *v.a.* give up 27, 722; leave off, turn away from 932
guerre, *sf.* warring 4, 1044*n*; sanz g. without resistance 1724
guerrëer 69, *v.a.* oppose, wage war on
guit, *subj.pr.3* of guier, *v.a.* to guide 132
gurz, *adj.nom.sg.m.* idle, sluggish 220
gutes, *s.pl.* drops 1681
gwardee *see* guarder

habit 1528; *nom.sg.* abit 655; *obl.pl.* habiz 31; *s.* dress, habit
haïr; *pret.3* haï 1281; *pp.* haït 1026; *v.a.* hate
hait, *s.* joy 668
haitément, *adv.* joyfully 1811
haitét, *pp.adj.nom.pl.m.* happy 1817
halcer; *v.a.* raise 1147; build up 1670; *v.n.* rise 1153
halt 1188, 1506, 1776; *nom.pl.m.* halt 255, 1695; *f.sg* halte 247, 1064, 1640, alte 481; *f.pl.* haltes 189; *adj.* high 247, 255, 481 *etc.*; open (*of sea*) 1064, 1640; loud 189; *adv.* high 521, 934, 936 *etc.*; loudly 557, 912, 1057 *etc.*
haltece, *sf.* height 493*n*, 1190
haltement, *adv.* loudly 453
han *see* ahan
hanap, *sm.* cup, chalice 315*n*
hanter; *v.a.* frequent, live in 1702*n*
haspes, *sm.pl.* hasps, clasps 686*n*
hastivement, *adv.* quickly 653, 1405
helte, *sm.* hilt 1709
herberger, *subst.inf.* lodging 307
herbes *see* erbe
heritét, *s.* heritage 51

hermite 1537, 1541, **ermite** 75, *s.* hermit

ho(e)m *see* **homme**

homme 1222, **hume** 278; *nom.sg.* **hom** 40, 500, 721 *etc.*, **hoem** 26, 243, 1173, **um** 960, 1273; *nom.pl.* **home** 1459; *sm.* man 40, 126, 278 *etc.*; *indef.pron.* one 243, 960, 1273, 1604

honeste, *adj.* honest 819

honurs, *s.pl.* honours 28

horribles, *adj.nom.sg.m.* terrifying 1331, 1344

hoste 825, 857, 878 *etc.*, **oste** 884, 1633, 1653; *sm.* host (*cf.* 356*n*)

hui 1429, **oi** 393, *adv.* today

humaine, *adj.f.* human 561; *cf.* **gent**

humlement, *adv.* humbly 659, 1724

hure *see* **ure**

i, *adv.* there 33, 108, 251 *etc.*; here 402, 422, 743 *etc.*; in it 179, 181, 184 *etc.*; (*pleonastic*) 1370; *pron.* in him 1180; to them 1521; *cf.* **aveir**

iceals, icel, icele, iceols *see* **cil**

icest, icez *see* **cist**

ici 68, 119, 330 *etc.*, **ci** 139, 417, 420 *etc.*; *adv.* here 68, 366, 417 *etc.*; here, to this place 473, 1428, 1547 *etc.*; (from) here 1326; **d'ici** from here 119, 330, 391 *etc.*; **de ci que** 139, 1102, **d'ici que** 648, *conj.* until; *see also* **aloeces, desque**[1], **enturn**

icil *see* **cil**

icist *see* **cist**

ičo *see* **čo**

idunc, *adv.* then, in these circumstances 228*n*

il (*unstressed*) *nom.sg.m.* 56, 61, 83 *etc.*; *acc.sg.m.* **le** 101, 148, 196 *etc.*, **l'** 317, 318, 336 *etc.*; *dat.sg.m.* **li** 47, 81, 139 *etc.*, **l'** (*only before* **en**) 115, 414, 1606, **lui** 49, 60, 71 *etc.*; *nom.pl.m.* **il** 64, 182, 372 *etc.*; *acc.pl.m.* **les** 149, 150, 153 *etc.*; *dat.pl.* **lur** 109, 126, 136 *etc.*, **lor**

378; *acc.sg.f.* **la** 177 *etc.*, **le** *cf.* 157*n*, **l'** 176, 837, 838 *etc.*; (*stressed*) *obl.sg.m.* **lui** 33*n*, 35, 37 *etc.*; *obl.pl.m.* **els** 124, 714, 1177 *etc.*; **eals** 151, 254, 577 *etc.*; *pers.pron.* he, him, it, they, them; (*enclitic*) *see* **jol, chis, eissil, las**[1], **nel, nes, ques, quis**[1], **sil, sis**[1], **tul**

ila, *adv.* there 1219; *cf.* **la**

ileoc 53, 66, 404 *etc.*, **iloc** 413, **iloces** 1363, 1367, **iloec** 126, 182, 294 *etc.*, **iloeces** 1417, *adv.* there; *cf.* **aloeces**

ire, *s.* torment 1385*n*

isle, *sm.* island 93, 97, 423, 1165*n etc.*

isselites, *pp.adj.f.pl.* choice, exquisite 1682

issent *see* **eissir**

issi *see* **eisi**

istrai *see* **eisir**

itant, *adv.* so 686, 1242, 1383, 1419; **itant . . . cum(e)** as . . . as 389, 490; **fors sul itant** this much 539*n*; *cf.* **tant, cum**

itel *see* **tel**

ivern 1240, 1330; *nom.sg.* **ivers** 421; *sm.* winter

ja, *adv.* now 188; **ne . . . ja** never 420, 1760; **ja seit ço que** although 1610; *cf.* **jamais**

jacinctes, *sm.nom.sg.* jacinth 1689*n*

jacoines, *sm.nom.sg.* great fish 837*n*

jadis, *adv.* once, formerly 520

jagunces *see* **jargunce**

jamais, *adv.*: **ne . . . j.** never again 1634; *cf.* **mais**[2]

jargunce 1065*n*, 1067, 1685*n*; *pl.* **jagunces** 683; *s.* jacinth

jaspes, *s.pl.* jasper 685, 1687*n*

jeter; *ind.pr.2* **gettes** 344, *3* **jetet** 461, 1207, 1232, *6* **gettent** 96; *pres.p.* **jetant** 1141; *v.a.* throw 344, 461, 1232; emit 1141, 1207; give off 96

jo (*unstressed*) *nom.sg.* 119, 432, 584 *etc.*; *obl.sg.* **me** 515, 1261, 1268, *etc.*, **m'** 120, 860, 1316 *etc.*; (*stressed*) *obl.sg.m.* **mei** 344, 460, 518

etc. (*cf.* also 1258, 1393, 1429 *etc.*);
pers. pron. I, me; *cf.* **nus**
jol 1473 = **jo** + **le**
jugement 1484, 1503, 1559; *nom.sg.*
jugemenz 1248; *sm.* judgement
1248, 1484, 1503; last judgement
1559
juine, *s.:* **faire j.** fast 132
juïse, *sm.* last judgment 1555, 1798
juner; *v.n.* fast 133
jurn 137, 745, 747 *etc.*; *nom.sg.*
jurz 1480, **jurn** 555; *obl.pl.* **jurs**
134, 219, 260 *etc.*, **jurz** 1663; *sm.*
day
jus, *adv.* down; *cf.* **descendre** 1070,
gesir 810, **metre** 385, **rüer** 1411; **en
jus** below 1348
jusdi, *sm.* Thursday 1389; **j. de la
ceine** 393*n*, 1611, **j. absolud** 822,
Maundy Thursday
justedes, *pp.f.pl.* of **juster**, *v.a.* clash,
come to blows 933
justes, *nom.sg.* 42; *obl.pl.* 1561; *adj.*
just, righteous 42; *s.* the just 1561
juvencel 1715; *nom.sg.* **juvenceals**
1729, 1805; *sm.* young man
juvenilz, *adj.obl.pl.m.* youthful 407

ki *see* **qui**
ki'n 1068 = **qui** + **en**

l', **la**, *see* **il**, **li**
la, *adv.* there 101, 130, 132 *etc.*; *cf.*
desque[1], **ila**, **las**[1]
laier; *fut.6* **lairunt** 1472; *imper.2* **lai**
193; *v.a.* allow; **ne l. que . . . ne** not
refrain from 1472
laiser; *ind.pr.6* **leisent** 567; *v.a.* leave
567, 959, 1469, 1475; end 507
lait, *s.* milk 1749
lamme 1143, **lame** 1159; *pl.* **lammes**
1124, 1127, 1208; *sf.* blade
lampes, *s.pl.* lamps 756, 1085
landes, *s.pl.* open country 390
larecin, *sm.* theft 319, 336*n*; **en l.** by
stealth 1272
larges, *adj.pl.* huge 1439
las[1] 1186*n* = **la** + **les**

las[2] 522; *f.* **lasse** 1264; *adj.* weary
1264; *s.* wretch 522
lascer; *v.a.* slacken 385
lassement, *adv.* wearily 1238
lassét, *pp.adj.nom.pl.* fatigued 573,
638
laver; *v.refl.* wash oneself 754
le *see* **il**, **li**
léd 1666, **liéd** 1819, *adj.* glad
ledement, *adv.* widely 497
ledes, *adj.f.pl.* broad 491
leger 695; *nom.sg.m.* **legiers** 1331;
adj. light (*in spirit*) 695; easy to
bear 1331
lei, *sf.* law 2, 3, 69; canon law 1036
leisent *see* **laiser**
leist, *ind.pr.3* of **leisir**, *v.impers.* be
permitted 1787
leres, *sm.nom.sg.* thief 334
lermes, *s.pl.* tears 892
les *see* **il**, **li**
letre, *s.* writing, Latin? 11*n*
leu 160, 263, 269 *etc.*, **liu** 86, 91, 431
etc., **lu** 63, 701, 1184; *nom.sg.* **leus**
666, **lius** 1323; *obl.pl.* **leus** 35, 727,
lius 1438; *sm.* place 63, 86, 91 *etc.*;
en lu de instead of 701
lever; *v.a.* raise 207, 1077, 1251; *v.n.*
l. sus get up 317; *v.pron.* **s'en l.** get
up from table 705
li *nom.sg.m.* 8, 12, 36 *etc.*, **l'** 203, 313,
321 *etc.*, **le** 123, 197, 543 *etc*;
obl.sg.m. **le** 6, 13, 24 *etc.*, **l'** 31, 141,
166 *etc.*, **lu** 5; *nom.pl.m.* **li** 62, 63,
92 *etc.*; *obl.pl.m.* **les** 28, 31, 45 *etc.*;
f.sg. **la** 1, 69, 99 *etc.*, **l'** 100, 178,
308 *etc.*; **le** 157*n* *etc.*; *pl.* **les** 5, 204,
213 *etc.*; *def. art.* the; that 444, 841,
1477; (during) each 134, 591,
1407; *cf.* **al**, **as**, **del**, **des**[1], **el**[1], **es**,
plus
liéd 1819 *see* **léd**
lïer; *pp.* **liéd** 1225, 1374; *v.a.* bind
1225, 1374; *v.refl.* wrap oneself
1442, 1451
lin, *sm.* family 21, 44
liois, *sm.* limestone 262
listes, *s.pl.* borders 1688

lit 1365; *nom.pl.* **liz** 571; *sm.* bed 571; **el l. metre** lay flat 1365
litur, *sm.nom.pl.* readers 698
liu(s) *see* **leu**
liuues, *s.pl.* leagues 465
liverer; *v.a.* deliver 603, 1286
loër 305, 376; *ind.pr.6* **loient** 1619; *v.a.* praise 305, 376, 565, 1619
lor *see* **lur, il**
loreür, *sm.* servant 743*n*
los, *s.* advice 79
lu *see* **leu, li**
lui *see* **il**
luin 165, 256, 382 *etc.*, **luign** 1109, 1170, 1326, 1696, **luinz** 242, 1630; *adv.* far 165, 242, 500 *etc.*; **de l.** from a distance 851, 1109; **en l.** far out 256; **de plus l.** on the horizon 382*n*
luiner; *ind.pr.3* **luinet** 784; *ind.impf.3* **luigneit** 456; *v.a.* carry away 784; *v.pron.* move away 456
luisir; *ind.pr.3* **luist** 1755, *6* **luisent** 1688; *v.n.* shine
lunc 785, 1159, 1539; *obl.pl.* **luncs** 461; *adj.* long 461; **l. tens** a long time 785, 1159, 1539
lundi *see* **lunsdi**
lunges, *adv.* for a long time 1511, 1609, 1770
lunsdi 1470, **lundi** 1353, *sm.* Monday
lur 152, 155, 156 *etc.*, **lor** 190, *poss.adj.* their 152, 155, 156 *etc.*, (+ *def.art.*) 1088; *poss.pron.* **la lur** theirs 887; *see also* **il**
lus, *s.pl.* wolves 1282
lutres, *sm.nom.sg.* otter 1565
lüur, *sf.* light 1417; brilliance 1679, 1693

m' *see* **jo**
ma *see* **mun**
maigre, *adj.* thin, lean 1023
mail, *sm.* hammer 1135
main[1], *s.* morning 579; *see also* **prime**
main[2], *sf.* hand 204, 658, 692 *etc.*
maine *see* **mener**

mairen 174, **mairein** 1066, *s.* timber, (building) material
mais[1] 14 *etc.*, **meis** 370, *conj.* but 14, 17, 47 *etc.*
mais[2] 953, 1117, **meis** 818, *adv.*: **ne . . . m.** never again 818; never 953; **unc m.** never before 1117; *see also* **jamais**
maisun, *sf.* house 274, 344
majestéd 540, **majestét** 1239, *sf.* majesty, glory
mal[1] 539, 549, 904 *etc.*; *nom.sg.* **mals** 738; *obl.pl.* **mals** 1352, 1412; *sm.* suffering, hardship, torment, evil
mal[2] 63 *etc.*; *nom.sg.* **mals** 94, 1447; *obl.pl.* **mals** 1760*n*; *adj.* cold, unfavourable (*of wind*) 94, 1760; harsh, painful 1390, 1430; *subst.adj.* evildoer 63; evil action 1447; *adv.* treacherously, to his cost 524
malfez 1133, 1202, 1478, **malsfeiz** 1167, *sm.* demon; *cf. also* **féd**
mander; *v.a.* command, summon 1547
mandét, *sm.* ritual washing of feet 829*n*, 877
mandrez *see* **maneir**
maneie, *s.* mercy, protection 225
maneir; *ind.impf.3* **maneit** 728; *fut.5* **mandrez** 861; *subj.impf.1* **mansisse** 772; *v.n.* live 728; remain 772, 861; *cf.* **remaindre**
manger 697, *v.a. and n.* eat 303, 568, 990; *subst.inf.* food, meal 450, 451
marbre 273, 490, 1695; *nom.* **marbres** 1383; *sm.* marble
marbrin, *adj.* of marble 1697
marin, *adj.* sea- 478, 905, 1571
mast, *sm.* mast 209, 611
mate, *adj.f.* dejected 1284
materie, *s.* substance 1674*n*
matin, *sm.*: **le m.** next morning 444, 841, 1183, 1470
matines, *s.pl.* matins 576
me *see* **jo**
mecredi, *sm.* Wednesday 1369
mei *see* **jo**

meilurs, *adj.m.obl.pl.* best 108
meilz *see* **mielz**
meindres *see* **menur**
mein(e)(n)t, **meineit**, **meinge** *see* **mener**
meis[1] *sm.* month 235, 588, 605 *etc.*
meis[2] 370 *see* **mais**[1]
meis[3] 818 *see* **mais**[2]
meistre, *s.* master 525, 528
meitez, *s.pl.* parts 950*n*
mel, *sm.* honey 1751
melodie, *s.* singing 1781
melz *see* **mielz**
men *see* **mun**
mendi, *adj.nom.sg.* beggar 1280
mener 155, 473, 662; *ind.pr.3* **meinet** 212, 267, 713 *etc.*, **maine** 439, **menet** 1525, 6 **meinent** 693, 1334; *ind.impf.3* **meineit** 1186; *fut.1* **menrai** 1786, *3* **menrat** 1599; *sbj.pr.1* **meinge** 119, *3* **meint** 115, 130; *pp.* **menét** 250, **menez** 125, 1291; *v.a.* lead, take (along), bring 115, 119, 125 *etc.*; show (*emotions*) 538; undergo 1334; *cf.* **demener**
mentet, *sbj.pr.3 of* **mentir**, *v.a.* break (*faith*) 298
menur 1236; *nom.sg.* **meindres** 1003; *adj.* smaller, less
mer, *sf.* sea 83, 90, 93 *etc.*; *cf.* **sal**
mercïer; *v.a.* give thanks (to) 558, 1491
mercit 338, 346, 1242, 1246, **merci** 306, *sf.* mercy, pity, forgiveness: **faire m.** a pardon 346
merite, *s.* deserts, due 64; merit, worth 1435
merveille, *s.* (cause for) wonder 419, 1342, 1710; marvel 475
merveiller 501, *v.n.* be astonished 472, 501; *v.a.* marvel at 1528
merveilles, *adv.* wondrously, exceedingly 380
mes[1], *sm.nom.* messenger 405; *cf.* **message**
mes[2], *s.pl.* cooked food 701
mes[3], *adj. see* **mun**

mescreance, *s.* lack of faith 1180
mescreire 243, 979, *v.n.* be lacking in faith
message, *sm.* messenger, angel 356, 724, 1717; *cf.* **mes**[1]
messes, *s.pl.* Masses 1088
mester 640, 801, 1117, 1578; *nom.sg.* **mesters** 286, 864; *obl.pl.* **mesters** 285; *sm.* kitchens 285; **estre m.** be useful, necessary 286, 640, 864; **aveir m.** have need 801*n*, 1117, 1578
mesure, *s.*: **sanz m.** without moderation 804; immeasurably 911
metre; *ind.pr.6* **metent** 229, 385, 891 *etc.*, **mettent** 1366; *imper.5* **metez** 225; *pret.3* **mist** 58, 90, 179 *etc.*, 6 **mistrent** 260, 447, 594; *pp.* **mis** 11; *v.a.* place, put 11, 58, 184 *etc.*; take (*time*) 260; appoint, set (*date*) 779, 891; *v.pron.* place oneself 225, 594; take to 229; put in 261, 666; **sei m. en** enter 281, 1657; come to 632; **sei m. en mer** put to sea 90; *see also* **fors**, **talent**
meüd *see* **muveir**
midi, *s.* midday 845, 1428
mie, *neg.part.*: **ne . . . mie** not all 1310, 1741, 1782
mielz 476, 819, **meilz** 105, **melz** 1171, *adv.* better 476 *etc.*; **de m.** the better 105; **cum m. pourent** as best they could 1171; *see also* **venir**
mil, *num.adj. and s.* thousand 7, 35, 914 *etc.*
millers, *s.pl.* thousands 1167
miracles, *s.pl.* miracles 374, 1001
mis *see* **metre** *and* **mun**
miserere, *s.* penitential psalm 707*n*
misericors, *adj.nom.sg.* merciful 1243
miserie, *sf.* suffering 1462
mist, **mistrent** *see* **metre**
moine 29, 78, 656, 687, 782, **muine** 813, 1078, 1091, 1489; *obl.pl.* **munies** 36, 107; *sm.* monk
mordanz, *pres.p.adj.pl.* sharp, cutting 939

mors 941, morz 1021, *s.pl.* bites
mort 348 *etc.; nom.pl.* morz 1400;
sf. death 910 *etc.; adj. and
subst.adj.m.nom.sg.* morz 1025, *f.*
morte 895, 948; dead 45 *etc.*;
motionless 895; *see also* murir
morz[1] *see* mort
morz[2] 1021 *see* mors
mot, moüs, move(n)t, moz*see* muveir
müer; *v.a.* change 1370, 1412
muilent, *ind.pr.6 of* moiller, *v.a.* wet,
soak 462
muine *see* moine
muit, *ind.pr.3 of* muire, *v.n.* roar 924,
1326
mult 18 *etc.; f.pl.* multes 1772;
obl.pl.m. mulz 1830; *adj.* many
614, 1459, 1772; *adv.* (very) much,
greatly 18, 201, 216 *etc.*; very 40,
87, 152 *etc.*; a long time 408; a
great distance 456; *pron.* many 33,
1682, 1830
mun 1091 *etc.; nom.sg.m.* mis 1386,
1592, mes 1420; *obl.pl.m.* mes
514, *etc.; f.sg.* ma 344 *etc.; f.pl.* mes
1275 *etc.; str.obl.sg.* men 749,
1380; *adj.* my 344 *etc.; pron.*: le
men mine 749*n*
muncel, *sm.* small mound 1457
mund 24, 1591, munde 1074, *sm.*
world
munies *see* moine
munt 1131, 1185, 1339, *etc.; nom.sg.*
munz 1190, 1205; *nom.pl(?)* munz
633; *sm.* mountain
muntaine, *sf.* mountain 1698
munter; *ind.impf.3* muntout 494,
1069; *v.n.* rise 494, 1069, 1349
mur 271, 1696; *nom.sg.* murs 1669,
1680, 1683 *etc.; sm.* wall
mure, *sf.* point (*of sword*) 1709
murét, *s.* sweetened wine 704
murget *see* murir
murir 1040, 1048, murrir 340;
ind.pr.3 mort 422; *fut.2* muras
776; *sbj.pr.3* murget 61; *v.n.* die;
cf. also mort
murs, *sm.pl.* way of life, morals 76

muster, *sm.* abbey 191, 726; church
706
mustrer 325, *v.a.* show, make known,
reveal 49, 60, 81 *etc.*
muveir (*Ms. muver*) 1614; *ind.pr.2*
moz 1241, 1322, 3 mot 1017, 1253,
1756, 6 movent 1621; *ind.impf.3*
muveit 455, 915; *pret.2* moüs 774;
fut.2 muveras 777, 4 muverum
392, 5 muverez 768; *sbj.pr.3* movet
1510; *pp.* meüd 191; *v.a.* move, stir
915, 1017, 1241, 1756; *v.n.* leave,
set out 191, 768, 774 *etc.*; be in
motion 455, 1253; move 1510;
v.refl. set out 392

nafrer, *v.refl.* wound each other 939
nager 216, 249, *v.n.* row 228, 235;
subst.inf. rowing 384
naisance, *s.* birth 20
naistre; *pret.2* nasquis 776; *pp.* néd
19; *v.n.* be born; *see also* nez
narine, *s.* nostril 935
nasquis *see* naistre
nature, *s.* nature, properties 649,
1783
naturel, *adj.* pure 1065
ne[1] 14 *etc.,* n' 16 *etc.,* nen 70, 242, 365
etc., neg.partic. not 16, 17, 26 *etc.*;
(*expletive*) 14, 566, 746, 752, 765,
902, 1231, 1424, 1472, 1546,
1792; *see also* nel, nes
ne[2] 70, 137, 422 *etc.,* n' 1240 *etc.,*
conj. and . . . not, nor 70 *etc.*;
ne . . . ne either . . . or 137 *etc.*
néd *see* naistre
nef, *sf.* ship 174, 180, 252 *etc.*
neif; *nom.sg.* neifs 1533; *obl.pl.* neifs
1675; *sf.* snow
neir, *adj.* black 1104, 1193
neïs, *adv.* (not) even 331
nel = ne + le 128, 435, 696 *etc.*
nen *see* ne[1]
nent *see* nient
nepuroec, *conj.* nevertheless 629; *cf.*
puroc
nepurtant, *conj.* nevertheless 55,
575, 627, 1099

nerçun, *s.* blackness 1107
nes = ne + les 1326
nez, *pp.subst.nom.sg.* son 1245; *cf.*
  naistre
nie, *sbj.pr.1 of* neier, *v.n.* drown
  1452*n*
nïent 1476, 1636, nent 981, *adv.* by
  no means 981; *pron.* nothing:
  ne faire n. be no question (of)
  1636; n'aveir n. be unsuccessful
  1476*n*
niule, *s.* cloud 1608
noble, *adj.* honourable, befitting roy-
  alty 22
noës, *sf.pl.* fins 937
noise, *sf.* noise 1047
nonante 1590, nunante 1553, *num.*
  adj. ninety
nostre 51, 459, 470 *etc.*; *obl.pl.f.* noz
  756; *adj.* our
noz *see* nostre
nuble, *s.* mist, cloud 1104
nublece, *s.* cloud 1185
nud, *adj.* naked 1222, 1450
nue, *sf.* sky, clouds 214, 496, 936
  etc.; cloud 1652, 1655, 1660
  etc.
nuit, *sf.* night 137, 322, 427 *etc.*
nul 135 *etc.*; *m.nom.sg.* nuls 92, 94,
  376 *etc.*, nul 254; *f.sg.* nul' 251,
  739, 1244 *etc.*, nule 332, 411, 762
  etc.; *pron.* (with neg) no one 92,
  135, 226 *etc.*; *adj.* any 236, 411,
  634 *etc.*; (with neg.) not . . . any, no
  251, 302, 762 *etc.*;(without neg.)
  630*n*, 786[1]
num *see* nun[1]
numbrer; *v.refl.* count themselves
  1493
numer; *v.a.* name 1523, 1720
nun[1] 75, 131, 1518, 1537, 1720,
  num 280, 543, *sm.* name: aveir n.
  be called 75, 1537
nun[2], *adv.* not 90, 653: se . . . n.
  unless, except 1376; si ço n. otherwise 1040
nunante *see* nonante
nune, *s.* mid-afternoon 1428*n*

nus, *pron.* we, us 52, 54, 58 *etc.*
nuvel; *nom.pl.* nuvels 1406; *obl.pl.*
  nuveals 828; *adj.* new
nuvele, *s.* news 1815

o 1795 *see* u[1]
obeïr 151; *pret.4* obedimes 532,
  obeïmes 732; *v.n.* obey
occean, *s.* ocean 166, 550
occident, *s.* West 212, 894
ocis, *pp. of* occire, *v.a.* kill 1032
od, *prep.* with 25, 73, 78 *etc.*: od tut
  together with 1486
odur 95; *obl.pl.* udurs 1738; *sm.*
  odour
odveoc *see* ovoec
öeile, *sf.* ewe, sheep 420
oënt *see* oïr
offrande, *s.* offerings, gifts 1273
offrir; *v.a.* offer 1295
oi *see* hui, aveir, oïr
oïd, oient, oïmes *see* oïr
oïde, *s.* hearing 100
oile, *s.* oil 758
oilz *see* uilz
oïr; *ind.pr.1* oi 1326, *3* ot 103, oit
  1249, *6* oënt 1168, oient 1779,
  1781; *pret.4* oïmes 727, 1046, *6*
  oïrent 111, 851; *pp.* oït 124, 1109,
  oïd 563, 1197; *v.a. and n.* hear 111
  etc.; *cf.* oïde
oiseil 611; *nom.sg.* oiseil 519; *nom.pl.*
  oisel 517, oiseals 852; *obl.pl.* oiseus
  499, 504, 508, 848, oiseals 850,
  868, 1623, oisals 578; *sm.* bird; *see*
  also Paraïs as Oiseus
oit 1249 *see* oïr
or, *sm.* gold 275, 291, 312 *etc.*; *see*
  also ore
orage, *s.* strong wind 793
orde, *adj.f.* foul 1415
ordre, *sm.* monastic rule, order 31,
  34, 733
ore 669, 1372, 1793, or 164, 371, 402
  etc., *adv.* now
oré; uré 1000; *nom.sg.* orez 1756,
  orrez 94, 211, 1254; *obl.pl.* orez
  1812; *sm.* wind

orguil, *s.* arrogance, arrogant behaviour 67, 538
orguillus, *adj.subst.* arrogant person (= Satan) 522
orïent, *s.* East 211, 1635
orrez *see* **oré**
orthie, *s.* nettle 1740
os¹, *sm.*: **aveir os a** be useful to 636
os² *s.* bone: **en carn e os** in flesh and blood 1557
oser 307; *ind.pr.1* **os** 1247; *v.n.* dare 254; venture? 307*n*, 414*n*
oste *see* **hoste**
ostét, *pp. of* **oster**, *v.a.* remove 1373
ot *see* **oïr**
otreid, *s.* authority, consent 1643
oüd *see* **aveir**
oür 362, 922; *nom.sg.* **oürs** 1176; *sm.* good fortune 1176; **bon o.** happiness 362, 922
ourent, ous-, out, oüt *see* **aveir**
ovoec 642 *etc.*, **oveoc** 65, **odveoc** 181, *prep.* (together) with 642, 1347, 1403, 1730; *adv.* also 65, 181, 1633

pain, *sm.* (loaf of) bread 357, 409, 603 *etc.*
paint *see* **pener**
païs, *sm.* country 409, 775, 1815; land 616; *cf.* **entrer**
pais, *s.* peace 280; **estre em p.** keep quiet 872
paisible, *adj.* calm 789
paistre 526; *ind.pr.3* **paist** 375; *pret.3* **pout** 1566; *pp.* **poüz** 95, **poüd** 1576, 1577; *v.a.* feed
palais 279, 281; *obl.pl.* **paleiz** 273; *sm.* great hall
palmes, *s.pl.* outstretched hands 190
palud, *s.* bog, marsh 791
pan, *s.* distance, stretch 480
par, *prep.* (*time*) for 219, 404, 785 *etc.*; by 322; on 1353; (*place*) in 35, 390, 497 *etc.*; through 168, 285, 1129 *etc.*; over, across 194, 379, 550 *etc.*; by 1513, 1664; **par tut** everywere 978, 1750; (*cause*) because of 33, 38, 57 *etc.*; (*means*) through, by (means of) 6, 72, 81 *etc.*; (*manner*) in, with 32, 154 *etc.*; **par lui, sei** on his own 759, 1523; **par vedue** 493*n*; *see also* **dreit, unt¹**
parain, *sm.* godfather 89
paraïs, *sm.* Paradise 49, 96, 99 *etc.*
pareir 382; *ind.pr.3* **pert** 1641, 1669, 6 **perent** 1447; *v.n.* appear, become visible
pareit, *sm.nom.pl.* walls 276
parent, *sm.* relative 159; family 1817
parfin, *sf.*: **a la p.** in the end 627
parfunt; *m.obl.pl.* **parfunz** 1123; *f.sg.* **parfunde** 1042; *f.pl.* **parfundes** 943; *adj.* deep 883*n*, 943, 1042, 1123; *adv.* **cliner p.** make a low bow 369, 659
parler 284 *etc.*, *v.n.* speak, talk 112, 284, 512 *etc.*
parmi, *adv.* through the middle 1658; *prep.* **p. tut ço** even so, for all that 462*n*
part 231 *etc.*; *obl.pl.* **parz** 1662; *sf.* **quel p.** in which direction 231, 233, 610; **icele p.** in that direction 383, 1075; **de (la) p. (de)** on behalf of 406, 1257; part 379, 982; side 1479, 1662
part, *ind.pr.3 of* **partir**, *v.n.* break, divide 1655
partint, *pret.3 of* **partenir**, *v.n.* belong to 1061*n*
pas, *neg.particle*: **ne . . . pas** not 469, 1472, 1787
pascal 400, **paschur** 843, *adj.*: **di paschur** Easter Day
passer 1652, *v.a.* pass through 574, 1652; *v.n.* pass over 1156*n*
past, *sm.* meal, food 991, 1570
paveiluns, *sm.nom.sg.* awning, tent 1071
pavemenz, *sm.nom.sg.* paving, pavement 1082
peccét 57; *obl.pl.* **pechez** 1200; *sm.* sin
peil 407, 1529, 1756; *nom.sg.* **peilz** 1534; *sm.* hair

peine, *sf.* difficulty 440, 1612; pain, suffering, torment 66, 394, 539 *etc.*

peiner, peine(n)t *see* **pener**

peinible *see* **penible**

peis[1], *s.* weight 606

peis[2], *s.: * **sur p.** reluctantly 1582*n*

peisance, *s.* grief, suffering 740

peissun 1062, **peisun** 833, 982, 1566 *etc.*; *nom.sg.* **pessuns** 471, **peisuns** 1618; *obl.pl.* **pessuns** 478, 799, **peissuns** 1044, 1045, **peisuns** 1569, 1573, 1577; *sm.* fish 471 *etc.*; sea-monster 982, 1044, 1045, 1062; whale 833, 1615, 1618

peiz, *sf.* pitch, tar 1209, 1371, 1379, 1381

pel[1], *sf.* skin 1402

pel[2], *s.* stake 1404

pelerin, *sm.* pilgrim 720, 854, 917, 1097, 1666

pendre; *ind.pr.3* **pent** 1707, 1711; *pret.1* **pendi** 1268; *pres.p.* **pendant** 256; *pp.* **pendud** 1571, **penduz** 1293; *v.n.* hang 256 *etc.*; *v.refl.* hang oneself 1268

pener 217, 238, **peiner** 1101; *ind.pr.3* **peinet** 1252, 6 **peinent** 216, 1100, 1333; *sbj.pr.3* **paint** 760; *pp.* **penét** 249; *v.a.* exert 217; *v.n.* toil, work hard 238, 1101; suffer 1333; *v.pron.* strive, toil 216, 1100, 1252; take pains, look after 760*n*; *adj.pp.* exhausted 249

penible; **peinible** 790; *nom.sg.* **penibles** 1332, 1343; *adj.* painful, grievous

penser 416, *v.a.* think, conceive of 127*n*, 416; *v.n.* **p. de** attend to, see to it that 398

pent *see* **pendre**

penus, *adj.* hard to bear, painful 1336

peot *see* **poeir**

percét, *pp.adj.* pierced through 1368

perches, *s.pl.* poles, rods 1208

perdre; *pres.p.* **perdant** 540; *v.a.* lose, be deprived of 213, 239, 835 *etc.*

pere[1] 1039 *etc.*; *nom.sg.* **peres** 146, 155, 354, 823; *sm.* father (*title of respect*) 1039, 1535, 1820

pere[2], *sf.* rock 1227, 1443; precious stone 677, 1754, 1799

perent *see* **pareir**

peril 258 *etc.*; *nom.sg.* **perilz** 1004, 1370, **peril** 1002; *obl.pl.* **perilz** 408, 574, 957, 1053; *sm.* peril, danger 258, 360, 408 *etc.*

perir; *ind.impf.6* **periseient** 1459; *sbj.pr.6* **perisent** 602; *pp.* **periz** 1223; *v.n.* perish, die 602 *etc.*; *pp.* doomed, lost 1223*n*

pernanz, pernez *see* **prendre**

pert *see* **pareir**

perte, *s.* loss 1619

pessuns *see* **peissun**

petiz, *adj.m.nom.sg.* small 169

pez, *s.pl.* feet 338, 657

piler 1064 *etc.*; *nom.sg.* **pilers** 1080; *sm.* pillar 1083, 1136, 1226

piu 1516; *m.nom.sg.* **pius** 36, 728, 1286 *etc.*; *m.nom.pl.* **piu** 92, 1600, 1736; *adj.* pious, holy 36 *etc.*; *subst.adj.* 92, 1600, 1736; Jesus 1286

plaies, *sf.pl.* wounds 943

plain *see* **plein**

plaindre 1249, *v.n.* lament, bewail

plaisir, *sm.* pleasure 130

plein 235 *etc.*, **plain** 210, *adj.* full, whole 235, 605, 998 *etc.*; **a p.** forthwith 210; completely 598

pleiner 1570; *f.sg.* **plenere** 1732; *m.obl.pl.* **pleiners** 1563; *adj.* whole 1563; abundant 1570; fertile 1732

pleintes, *s.pl.* laments 1238

plenere *see* **pleiner**

plentét, *sf.* plenty, abundance 290, 293, 504 *etc.*

plout, *pret.3 of* **plaisir**, *v.n.* please 303, 1500

pluius, *adj.* rainy 971

plum, *sm.* heavy weight 1366; lead 1410

plurer 1261; *ind.impf.3* **plurout** 1439; *v.n.* cry, weep 154, 333; *subst.inf.* 1261

plurs, *s.pl.* tears 609, 1439; lamentation 1168

plus, *adv.* more 26, 48, 88 *etc.*; longer 845, 1583; further 1191, 1192; most 288, 382, 1764; best 1172; **le p.** any the more 758*n*; **cum p. . . . (e) p.** the more . . . the more 1100, 1121, 1153; *cf.* **cum**

plusurs, *adj.* many 81, 727, 1167 *etc.*; more 1173*n*, 1834; *pron.* **li p.** the greater number, most 1827

podes 938, **poës** 1010, *sf.pl.* paws

poeir; *ind.pr.1* **puis** 1247, 1421, *3* **peot** 15, 17, **poet** 1632, 1783, **poit** 1386, **pot** 1714, **pout** 245, 382, *4* **poüm** 397, *6* **poient** 979, 1782; *pret.3* **pout** 180, 606, 1189, 1261, *6* **pourent** 238, 1171; *sbj.pr.3* **puisset** 600, 616; *sbj.impf.1* **pouse** 1573, *3* **poust** 1652; *v.n.* be able; *cf. also* **mielz**

poës *see* **podes**

poëstis, *adj.m.nom.sg.*: **estre p. de** be lord of 1646

poet *see* **poeir**

poi 414 *etc.*; *f.* **poie** 1768; *adj.* short 1768; *adv.* not very much, little 414, 1220, 1446, 1543, 1788; **pur (un) p.** almost, very nearly 752, 1014, 1231, 1424; **p. en falt . . . que ne** it is touch-and-go whether 901*n*; *pron.* **un p.** a little 859, 1325

poi(en)t *see* **poeir**

por *see* **pur**

port, *s.* harbour, port 167, 259, 261 *etc.*

portant, *pres.p.adj.*: **vent p.** favourable wind 893, 1163

porte, *sf.* entrance, doorway 1703

porter 180 *etc.*, *v.a.* carry, bring 180, 182, 357 *etc.*; take 295, 330, 1096, 1601, 1799; *cf. also* **en²** *and* **portant**

pose, *s.*: **estre en p.** stop, rest 1108; **p. del jurn** for a great part of the day 1371

post, *sm.* post 1374, 1375

pot, poüm *see* **poeir**

poüd *see* **paistre**

poür, *sf.* fear 921, 1175; **aveir p.** be afraid 240, 361, 468 *etc.*

pourent, pouse, poust, pout *see* **poeir**

pout 1566, **poüz** *see* **paistre**

povres, *adj.subst.obl.pl.* the poor 1274, 1279

praierie, *sf.* meadow, field 1733

precïus 1073; *f.pl.* **precïuses** 678; *adj.* costly 678, 1073; priceless, rare 1738*n*

préd Nerunt *see* **Nerunt**

pregnent *see* **prendre**

preiez, *pp.m.nom.sg. of* **preier**, *v.a.* snatch away 1199

preïstes *see* **prendre**

prement, *ind.pr.6 of* **prembre**, *v.a.* keep in check 652*n*

premseir, *sm.* (early) evening 1463

prendre 234 *etc.*; *ind.pr.1* **prenc** 1304, *3* **prent** 48, 73, 123 *etc.*, *6* **pregnent** 307, 1162, **prengent** 629, **prengnent** 596, 608, **prennent** 68, 440, **prenent** 800; *fut.3* **prendrat** 79, *5* **prendrez** 368; *pret.1* **pris** 1542, *3* **prist** 31, 39, 47 *etc.*, *5* **preïstes** 752, *6* **prestrent** 302, **pristrent** 448, 805, 807; *sbj.pr.1* **prenge** 120, *3* **prenget** 352, *6* **prengent** 1472; *imper.2* **prenges** 514, *5* **prengez** 296, **pernez** 399, 459, 993; *pres. p.obl.pl.* **pernanz** 37; *pp.* **pris** 71, 1248, 1803; *v.a.* take 31 *etc.*; set (*course*) 234, 1112; seize, capture 348, 1010, 1468; make (*land*) 440, 629; pay (*attention*) 514; pass (*judgement*) 1248; comprehend 1783*n*; **p. decés, sa fin** die 719 736; *v.n.* begin 48*n*, 307*n*, 868*n*; **p. a** begin 284, 501, 596; *v.impers.* **p. talent, desir a** be taken by the desire (to) 47, 71; *v.pron.* begin 120*n*; catch (*fire*) 1379; *see also* **achant, cunseil, cure, escuil, fuite, purpens**

pres, *adv.* near, close (to) 97, 378, 430 *etc.*

presence, *sf.* presence, manifestation 541

prest, *adj*. ready 395, 725, 745 *etc*.;
    ripe 1746
prestement, *adv*. readily 396, 955
prestre, *sm.nom.sg*. priest 208
prestrent 302 *see* **prendre**
prïer 43, 48; *ind.pr.3* **prïed** 65;
    ind.impf.3 **prïout** 813; *v.a. and n*.
    beg, ask 115, 329; pray 59, 65, 205
    etc.
prïere, *sf*. prayer 507
prime, *adj*.: **en p. main** first thing in
    the morning 579; *cf. also* **primes**
primers,   *adj.m.nom.sg*.   1003;
    m.obl.pl. 1575; first 1003, 1575;
    s.: **tut en p.** first of all 1669
primereine, *adj.f*. first 948
primes, *adv*. first 50, 73, 477 *etc*.:
    dunc, puis a p. and only then 768,
    770, 1559
pris(t), pristrent *see* **prendre**
prïur, *sm*. prior 149
processïun, *s*. procession 690
prometre; *ind.pr.3* **promet** 412, 6
    promettent 121; *v.a*. promise
propre, *s*.: **de p. . . . bien** personal
    property 1456*n*
pruver; *v.a*. prove 373
psalmodie, *s*. singing (of psalms) 570
puante, *pres.p.adj.f*. stinking 1106
pui, *sm*. hill, mountain 172, 255
puier; *v.a*. climb 1511
puin, *s*. fist 1135
puint 979 *etc*., **punt** 331, *sm*. scrap, bit
    331; *neg.particle*: **ne . . . p.** not
    (nothing) at all 979, 1402, 1579
puis, *adv*. then 32, 91, 101 *etc*.; *prep*.
    after 587, 625, 1581; *conj*.: **puis
    que** after, when 124, 319, 445
puisset *see* **poeir**
pullenz, *adj.m.nom.sg*. stinking 1346
puncel, *sm*. footbridge 1458
punt *see* **puint**
pur 21 *etc*., **por** 5, *prep*. because of, on
    account of 5, 122, 222, *etc*.; as 816,
    1050 *etc*.; on behalf of 44, 45, 297
    etc.; (in exchange) for 28, 722,
    1074; (*with neg*.) for (all), despite
    215, 323, 332; in the name of 244;

to the point of 1269*n*; in order to
    29, 448, 662 *etc*.; **p. quei** why 58,
    428, 468 *etc*., because of which
    258, 790, 808 *etc*.; **p. ço** for this
    reason 533, 1632; *conj*.: **p. ço, cel
    . . . que** because 21, 117, 299, 473,
    518; **p. ço que** in order that 986; *see
    also* **poi**, *and cf*. **puroc**
purcusent, *ind.pr.6 of* **purcusdre**, *v.a*.
    stitch over 597
puroc 22 *etc*., **puroec** 1461, *conj*. for
    this reason 27, 240, 243, 975,
    1276; *conj*.: **p. que** because 527; *cf*.
    nepuroec
purpens, *sm*. plan 109; resolve 1005:
    prendre (en) p. resolve, decide 39,
    1089
purplantez,   *pp.adj.m.nom.sg*.   set,
    covered 1680
purvëeir; *ind.pr.3* **purveit** 196; *pret.3*
    purvit 197, 300; *v.a*. foresee
purvit *see* **purvëeir**
püur 1169, 1418; *nom.sg*. **püurs**
    1419; *sf*. stench
puz, *sm.nom.sg*. pit 1120

quai *see* **quei**
quanque, *pron*. whatever 293, 416,
    1632; *adj*. (?) 1824*n*
quant[1], *conj*. when 84, 103, 111 *etc*.;
    since, seeing that 15, 325, 402 *etc*.;
    adv. when 715
quant[2], *pron*.: **tant q.** as far as 161
quar 325 *etc*., **quer** 46, 91, 97 *etc*.,
    conj. for, since 325, 455, 598 *etc*.;
    (*reinforcing imperative*) now, just
    454
quarante, *num.adj*. forty 183, 1592,
    1640 (*cf*. 631)
quarel, *sm*. bolt 1151
quarenteine, *sf*. period of forty days
    133
quart, *num.adj*. fourth 328, 1665
quatorze, *num.adj*. fourteen 107, 156
quatre, *num.adj*. four 625 (*cf*. 717)
que[1] 18 *etc*., **qu'** 53 *etc*., **q'** 897, *conj*.
    that 18, 23, 49 *etc*.; than 183, 566,
    765 *etc*.; for 900, 1386, 1546;

because 155; with the result that
1402; so that 132, 177, 600 *etc.*;
que . . . ne lest 818, 921, 1228 *etc.*,
without 1472, 1569*n*, 1641; since
719, 736; when 1244*n*, 1575,
1831; that, during which 1553,
1596, 1618 *etc.*; *cf.* **quel¹, ques**
que² *pron. see* **qui**
quei 58 *etc.*, **quai** 1256, *pron.*: **pur q.**
on account of which 58, 218, 258
etc., why 428, 468, 1051 *etc.*; *cf.*
also **qui**
quel¹ 1258 = **que + le**
quel² 62 *etc.*; *m.nom.sg.* **quels** 1336;
adj. which, what 63, 64, 232 *etc.*; **q.**
part in which direction 231, 233,
610 *etc.*: *pron.* which 1336, 1448;
whom 146
quelque, *adj.*: **q. . . . que** whatever
360, 976, 992
quer¹, *sm.* heart 142, 416, 1420, 1448
quer² *conj. see* **quar**
querre 84, 260, 285, *etc.*, **querre** 449,
773; *imper.4* **querums** 640; *pret.2*
quesis 543, *3* **quist** 1826, *6* **quis-**
trent 259; *pres.p.* **querant** 363; *pp.*
quis 665, 1596; *v.a.* ask after, seek
1090 *etc.*
ques 115 = **que + les**
quesis *see* **querre**
qui, *pron.*: *m. and f.nom.* 6, 17, 40
etc., **ki** 24, 988, 1032 *etc.*, **que**
(= **qui**) 38, 292, 598, 726, 802 *etc.*,
qu' 1332, **chi** 857, 894, 1138 *etc.*;
nom.neut. **que** 300, 640, 1061; *m.*
and f.obl. **que** 96, 104, 108 *etc.*, **qu'**
102, 136, 312 *etc.*; (*after prep.*) **qui**
2, 3, 581 *etc.*; *obl.neut.* **que** 9, 15,
246 *etc.*, **qu'** 83 *etc.*; *dat.* **qui** 581,
1478, 1637; who 17 *etc.*; he who 24
etc.; they who 249; whom 2 *etc.*; he
whom 439, 923; which, that 6 *etc.*;
that which, what 9 *etc.*; whose 581,
1478, 1637; **que que** whatever 361,
however much 1387; *cf. also* **chis,
ki'n, quei, quis¹**
quider (**quïer**); *ind.pr.5* **quïez** 566, *6*
quïent 1216, **quident** 1333;

ind.impf.1 **quidoue** 1277; *v.a.*
think, imagine
quinze, *num.adj.* fifteen 219, 912
quinzeine, *sf.* fifteen days 897, 1307*n*
quir, *sm.* hide 176, 597; skin 1406,
1423
quire 448, 1573, *v.a.* cook
quis¹ 212 = **qui + les**
quis², quist(rent) *see* **querre**
quite, *adj.* released, free 1436, 1538
quivere 1421, **quivre** 1410*n, sm.*
copper

racine, *s.* edible root 701
raëncune, *s.*: **faire r.** be unpleasant
(*of weather*) 421
rage, *sf.* fury, madness 930, 1298
raisun, *s.* reason 343
raler; *ind.pr.1* **revoi** 860; *pret.3* **realat**
952, **ralat** 1552, 1832; *imper.2*
reva 1797; *v.n. and pron.* return,
go back
raps, *sm.pl.* ropes 461
realat *see* **raler**
receivre 358, 604, 766; *ind.pr.3* **receit**
168, 195, 1210, 1719, *4* **recevum**
756; *pret.3* **receut** 347, 354; *fut.6*
recevrunt 64; *pp.* **reçoüd** 1178, *f.*
receüe 104; *v.a.* receive 64 *etc.*;
suck back in 1210*n*
recharger; *v.a.* reload 846
rechrie, *sbj.pr.3 of* **recrïer**, *v.a.* give
off, exude 1742
reclaim, *sm.* prayer 820
reclamer; *v.a.* call upon 458
reclin, *sm.* bed 320
reçoüd *see* **receivre**
recrerrunt, *fut.6 of* **recreire**, *v.n.*
desist (from) 1101
refait, *pp.m.nom.pl.* refreshed 705
refraitur 697, **refreitur** 710, *s.* refec-
tory
refreiz, *s.pl.* singing, responses? 577
refrigerie, *s.* mitigation, alleviation
1461
regal, *adj.* royal 21, 269; *cf.* **reials**
regne, *sm.* kingdom 534, 1833
regretter; *v.a.* implore 230

reguard 1137, 1531; *pl.* **reguarz** 1438; *sm.* look 1137, 1531; qualms, fear 1438

reguarder; *v.n.and pron.* look back, round 1164, 1204

rei 5, 1643; *nom.sg.* **reis** 477, 562, 1241, 1676; *sm.* king 19 *etc.*

reials, *adj.m.nom.sg.* royal 27; *cf.* **regal**

reïne, *sf.* queen 1

religïus, *adj.* devout 1516

reliques, *s.pl.* relics 674

remanance, *s.* dwelling place 952

remaindre; *ind.impf.3* **remaneit** 323; *fut.3* **remandrat** 4; *pret.3* **remist** 1809; *v.n.* remain, stay 1809; come to an end 4; *v.impers.* not happen, fail: **pur tenebres ne remaneit** this happened despite the darkness 323; *cf.* **maneir**

remis, *pp. of* **remetre**, *v.a.* melt 1384, 1410

remist *see* **remaindre**

remüers, *s.pl.*: **a r.** as replacements 599*n*

rendre; *ind.pr.3* **rent** 74, 337, 948, 1606, 6 **rendent** 1028; *pret.1* **rendi** 1299; *v.a.* render, make 948; give, acknowledge 1028, 1606; *v.pron.*: **sei r. confés** make one's confession 74, 337, 1299

rente, *s.* payment 1296

repairer; *ind.pr.1* **repair** 1358; *pret.3* **repairat** 590, **reparat** 823; *v.n.* return 590 *etc.*; live 1736

reparat 823 *see* **repairer**

repentance, *s.* repentance 1297

repentir, *subst.inf.* regret, repentance 120*n*

repleniz, *pp.m.nom.pl.* filled 1747

repos, *sm.* rest 350 *etc.*; respite 1303, 1318, 1432

reposer 308, 966; *ind.pr.1* **repos** 1429; *ind.impf.3* **reposout** 321; *v.a., n. and pron.* rest 638, 1527 *etc.*

repost, *pp.subst.*: **en r.** surreptitiously 318

reprent, *ind.pr.3 of* **reprendre**, *v.a.* recover 1154

requerre; *pret.2* **requeïs** 1790, *3* **requist** 101; *v.a.* seek out, visit 101; ask for, request 1790

resembler; *v.n.* appear, resemble 269

resirent, *pret.6 of* **reséeir**, *v.n.* take one's place, sit in one's turn 710*n*

resortet, *ind.pr.3 of* **resorter**, *v.n.* turn away (from) 1095*n*

resortir; *ind.pr.3* **resort** 257, 6 **resortent** 1694, *v.n.* swirl up 257; reflect 1694

respiz, *sm.pl.* exemplary sayings 82

respundre; *ind.pr.3* **respunt** 419, 519, 578 *etc.*, 6 **respundent** 113, **respunent** 961; *pret.3* **respundit** 415; *v.a.* answer, reply 773, 1323 *etc.*

respuns, *s.* reply 667

resusciter; *v.n.* rise again 1561

retenement, *s.* delay, holding back 1812

retenir 1725; *imper.5* **retenez** 646; *v.a.* restrain 1725; *v.refl.* get, hold back 646

retruver; *v.a.* find again 838

return, *s.* return journey 1597; **aveir r.** have recourse, help oneself 1648

returner; *v.refl.* turn back 1785

reva 1797 *see* **raler**

reveler; *v.n.* rebel 523

revenir 891; *ind. pr.1* **revenc** 1399, *3* **revent** 1405; *fut.2* **revendras** 775, 1794, 1796, 1797, *5* **revendrez** 429, 6 **revendrunt** 1634; *pret.3* **revint** 320, 1143, 1581, 6 **revindrent** 815; *v.n.* come back, return 429 *etc.*; grow again 1405; *subst.inf.* return 891; *see also* **sens**

revestud, *pp. of* **revestir**, *v.a.* robe, dress in vestments 687

revisder; *v.a.* visit 592

revoi 860 *see* **raler**

riche, *adj.* mighty, splendid 268, 270; precious 316; prosperous, rich 721, 1068, 1280

rien, *sf.* thing 47, 277, 1772; *pron.* anything 286, 411, 485 *etc.*;

neg.particle: **ne** . . . **r.** nothing 330, 656, 863 *etc.*; *cf.* **altre**

rivage, *sm.* shore 355, 368, 794, *etc.*

rive, *sf.* shore 1191, 1507

rivere, *s.* open country, meadow 1731

roceit *see* **rocheit**

roche, *sf.* rock 1128, 1214, 1215 *etc.*

rocheit 264, 633, **rochét** 1513, 1522, **roceit** 163; *obl.pl.* **rocheiz** 253; *sm.* rock

roe, *sf.* wheel 1354

roie, *adj.f.* harsh, hoarse 1264

roiste, *adj.* steep 1508

romanz, *s.* French 11

rosast, *sbj.impf.3 of* **reüser**, *v.a.* push back 1228*n*

rost, *s.* roast 1373

rove(n)t *see* **ruver**

rue, *sf.* roadway 1656

rüer; *v.a.* hurl, dash 1148, 1369, 1381, 1411

ruge 492, 1144; *nom.sg.* **ruges** 1377; *adj.* red

ruistes 1058, **rustes** 41*n*, *adj.pl.* stern, earnest 41; powerful, violent 1058

runceie, *s.* bramble-thicket 1739

ruseie, *sf.* reed-bed 1751*n*

ruseit, *sm.* dew 1752*n*

rustes *see* **ruistes**

rute, *s.* way 1502

ruver; *ind.pr.3* **rovet** 358, *4* **ruvum** 401, 746, *6* **rovent** 1108; *pret.3* **ruvat** 1824; *v.a.* ask, beg

s' *see* **se**[1], **si**[2]

sa *see* **sun**

sacel, *sm.* satchel, small bag 1572

sachez, **sachum** *see* **saveir**

sacraires, *sm.nom.sg.* shrine 1081

sage, *adj.* appropriate, as befits a wise man 1297

sai *see* **saveir**

sailir; *ind.pr.3* **salt** 935, 941, 1196, 1468, *6* **sailent** 386, 965, 1058; *v.n.* spurt out 935, 941; leap 1058, 1468; **s. sus, fors** jump out, disembark 386, 965, 1196; *cf. also* **sus**

sain, *adj.* wholesome 700

saint 13 *etc.*; *m.nom.sg.* **seinz** 19, **sainz** 98, 208, 847 *etc.*; *obl.pl.* **sainz** 1804; *f.sg.* **sainte** 76, 672; *adj.* holy, pious 76, 208, 672 *etc.*; saint 13, 98, 720 *etc.*; *sm.* saint 19, 847, 1804; *see also* **Saint Espirit**

saisir; *v.a.* provide (with), put in possession (of) 369

saisun, *s.* season 1744

sal, *s.*: **la mer de s.** the salt sea 1340; *cf.* **sel**

salt *see* **sailir**

salud, *s.* escape, safe deliverance, preservation (*from death*) 792

salüer; *v.a.* greet 7, 406

salz, *s.pl.* leaps, bounds 1142; *see also* **Salt Brandan**

samadi 405, 832, 1304, 1615, **samedi** 1411, 1427, *sm.* Saturday

sanc 1292; *nom.sg.* **sanz** 941; *sm.* blood

sanz[1], *prep.* without 235, 238, 250 *etc.*; **s. (ço) que** *conj.* without 746, 1558

sanz[2] 941 *see* **sanc**

saphire, *adj.* sapphire-blue 1067

sapin, *adj.*: **fust s.** pinewood 175

sardines, *s.pl.* sards, precious stones 683

sardoine, *s.* sardonyx, precious stone 1081, 1686

saüler; *v.a.* satiate, fill 702

saüls, *adj.m.nom.sg.* fully supplied, satiated 1588

saveir 527, 1433; *ind.pr.1* **sai** 414, 766, 1246, 1437, *3* **set** 15, 1095, 1120 *etc.*, *4* **savum** 128, 416, 649 *etc.*, *5* **savez** 467, *6* **sevent** 231, 795, 1098 *etc.*; *ind.impf.3* **saveit** 1630; *fut.3* **savrat** 26, 110, 1760; *pret.1* **soi** 1544, *3* **sout** 23, 158, 335, 1499, *6* **sourent** 1172, 1195; *sbj.impf.4* **sousum** 763; *imper.4* **sachum** 1218, *5* **sachez** 1048, 1115, 1290, 1503; *pres.p.* **savant** 1030, 1518, 1788; *v.a. and n.* know 15, 23, 128 *etc.*; know how, be able 26, 416, 1172, 1544; **s. fin** stop, reach the end

1098; *adj.pres.p.* informed 1030, 1518*n*, of sufficient understanding, fit 1788; *subst.inf.* knowledge, power 527, 1433; *see also* soüt

savie (= **saive**), *adj.* wise 1708*n*

savurét, *adj.* full-flavoured, sweet 700, 703

se[1] 34, 74, 90 *etc.*, **s'** 157, 165, 210 *etc.*; *str.obl.* **sei** 44, 58, 73; *refl. pron.* himself, oneself, themselves

se[2] *conj. see* **si**[2]

seant *see* **sedeir**

sec 1572, **secc** 968, *adj.* dry 1572; *sm.*: **al s.** on dry land 968*n*

secle, *sm.* world, earthly life 30, 1541, 1829

secrei, *sm.* secret, mystery 1090

secund, *prep.* according to 10, 805, 1543

séd *s.* abode, place in heaven 62

sedeillus, *adj.* dying of thirst 645

sedeir 1770, **setheir** 56; *pres.p.* **seant** 1222; *v.n.* sit; *subst.inf.* sitting 1429; *cf. also* **resirent**

seduit, *ind.pr.3 of* **seduire**, *v.a.* seduce 310

sëez *see* **estre**[1]

segur, *adj.nom.pl.* secure 1490; *cf.* **soür**

segut *see* **sivre**

sei[1] 332, 1602, **seif** 652, 1174, **seid** 788, 805, **seit** 1762, *sf.* thirst

sei[2] *pron. see* **se**[1]

seid, **seif** *see* **sei**[1]

seie(s), **seient** *see* **estre**[1]

seign, *sm.* guidance 594

seignacle 1807; *obl.pl.* **signacles** 1212; *s.* sign of the cross

seigne, *sm.* sign, beckoning 663*n*

seigner; *ind.pr.3* **seignet** 1251, **signet** 208; *v.a.* bless, make the sign of the cross over

seignur 524, 960, 1267 *etc.*; *nom.sg.* **sire** 1068, 1574; *nom.pl.* **seignurs** 127, 329, 334 *etc.*, **seignur** 690, 1199; *sm.* lord, master 524, 960, 1267; (= monks) 690; owner

1068; (*title of address*) 127, 329, 334 *etc.*

seinz *see* **saint**

seir, *s.* evening 1430

seisante, *num.adj.* sixty 1589

seit[1] *see* **estre**[1]

seit[2] 1762 *see* **sei**[1]

seivrement, *s.* separation 1560

sel, *sm.* salt 1403, 1408; *cf.* **sal**

semaine, *sf.* week 134, 591, 777 *etc.*

semblant, *s.* outward appearance 992; pretence 1269

sembler; *v.n.* seem, resemble 518, 1076, 1516, 1768

sen *see* **sens**

senés, *adv.* immediately 1431

senestre, *s.* left 1234

senez, *adj.pp.nom.sg.* wise, intelligent 126

senglantes, *pres.p.adj.f.pl.* bloody 944

sens 10 *etc.*, **sen** 1091, *sm.* wisdom, intelligence 40; wise course of action 110; opinion, understanding 1091; **secund sun (le) sens** to the best of his (my) ability 10, 1543; **revenir en lur s.** come to, recover consciousness 815

sentir 72; *subj.pr.1* **sente** 1396; *v.a. and pron.* experience, feel

seon(s) *see* **sun**

sepulture, *s.* burial 351

serf, *sm.* servant 74

sergant, *sm.* servant 1563

seril, *sm.* evening 1304

serir, *sm.* evening 1315

sermuner; *v.n.* preach, exhort 977

serpenz, *sm.nom.sg.* sea-serpent 905

serrer 596, *v.a.* cover thickly 496; propel 983; make watertight 596

serree, *pp.adj.f.* thick 1661

servant 16; *nom.sg.* **servanz** 1618; *nom.pl.* **servant** 371; *sm.* servant

servir 152, 960, 1096, *etc.*; *ind.impf.1* **serveie** 1265, 1544; *pret.4* **servimes** 531, 731, 6 **servirent** 709; *v.a. and n.* serve

servise, *sm.* religious service 443, 445, 695, 1035

ses *see* sun

set[1], *num.adj.* seven 866*n*, 874, 1596, 1617

set[2] *v. see* saveir

setheir *see* sedeir

seüd *see* sivre

sevent *see* saveir

si[1], *adv.* so, thus 219, 428, 737 *etc.*; such 504, 1117, 1462 *etc.*; *conj.* and (then) 284, 1218, 1219 *etc.*; then 553, 881, 1000 *etc.*; so 528; yet 914; **e si** and 195, 358, 1268, 1340, 1773, 1779, 1823; **si cum(e)** (just) as, like 54, 166, 482 *etc.*; as if 1214, 1530; as, when 1505; since 1427; *see also* **sil**, **sis**[1]; *cf.* **cum**

si[2] (=**se**) 110, 286, 411, 513, 1003, 1040, 1047, 1246, 1337, 1433, 1435, 1651, 1710, 1753, 1754, **s'** 414, **se** 798, 1376, 1384, *conj.* if, whether; **cume si** 1377, **cume se** 798 as if; *see also* **nun**[2]

sigle, *sm. and f.* sail 1077, 1654, 1808

sigler 896, *v.n.* sail 227, 377, 430, 435, 621, 833, 1075, 1609

signacles *see* seignacle

signet 208 *see* seigner

sil = **si** + **le** 528, 914; *cf.* **si**[1]

simple, *adj.* innocent 1282

sire *see* seignur

sis[1] = **si** + **les** 195, 358, 1049, 1340 1779; *cf.* **si**[1]

sis[2], *num.* six 547

sis[3] 1176, 1810 *see* sun

siste, *num.adj.* sixth 628

sivre; *ind.pr.1* **siu** 432; *imper.2* **siu** 1599; *pp.* **seüd** 192, **segut** 1562; *v.a.* follow

soen(s) *see* sun

soi *see* saveir

soleil, *sm.* sun 579, 1755, 1758

soleir; *ind.pr.3* **solt** 765; *ind.impf.6* **soleient** 1613; *v.n.* be accustomed

son *see* sun

soner; *v.n.* sound 509; *v.a.* ring 711

sor, *adj.* brightly coloured, red 682

soür 359; *m.nom.sg.* **süurs** 1765; *m.obl.pl.* **soürs** 116; *adj.* sure, secure; *cf.* **segur**

sourent, sousum, sout *see* saveir

soüt, *pp.subst.*: **tut a s.** for certain 373

spiritalment, *adv.* in the spirit 1796

streiz *see* estre[1]

süaté, *s.* sweetness 1742

sucurs 289, **succurs** 716, 957, *sm.* help 957; supply (*of food*) 289, 716

succurre; *ind.pr.3* **succurt** 793, 989; *fut.1* **succurrai** 864; *v.a.* succour, come to the help of

suduines, *adj.m.obl.pl.* besotted, drunk 814

süe(s) *see* sun

süef, *adv.* gently 487, 512, 1551; sweetly 1755; *adj.* clement, mild 1745

süer 1292, *v.a.* give off, exude 1751

sufflanz, *pres.p.adj.m.obl.pl.* blowing 1125, 1378

suffraite, *s.* privation 1762

suffrir 606, 819, 1328, 1390, 1782; *ind.pr.2* **suffres** 1256, *3* **suffret** 1426; *fut.5* **suffreiz** 549; *pret.3* **suffrit** 394; *pp.* **suffert** 546, 1053; *v.a.* endure, undergo, suffer

sufre, *s.* brimstone 1209

sui *see* estre[1]

suie, *sf.* soot 1403

sujurn, *sm.* rest 587, 1306, 1598; place of rest 873

sujurner 162, *v.n.* stay, rest 327, 769, 876, 1624

sul 1012, 1013, 1198 *etc.*; *m.nom.sg.* **suls** 1335; *adj.* alone, only 1012, 1013, 1198; **fors s.** except (only) 92, 283, 442 *etc.*; **uns suls** a single one 1335; *adv.* merely 1012*n*

sullenz, *adj.m.nom.sg.* damp, sweaty 1345

sultif, *adj.* solitary 88

sulunc, *prep.* according to: **siglez s.** sail down the wind 227

sumes *see* estre[1]

sumét, *sm.* summit 495, 1072

sumnes, *sm.nom.sg.* sleep 809

sun 10 *etc.*, **son** 84; *m.nom.sg.* 1176, 1810; *obl.pl.* **ses** 107, 145, 242 *etc.*; *f.sg.* **sa** 38, 174, 298; *f.pl.* **ses** 475, 506, 674, *etc.*; *str.m.obl.sg.* **soen** 105, 109, **seon** 144, 147, **son** 750*n*, **sun** 995, 1013, 1648; *str.m.obl.pl.* **soens** 283, **seons** 116, 206; *str.f.sg.* **süe** 1230; *str.f.pl.* **sües** 1210*n*; *adj.* his 10 *etc.*; its 869 *etc.*; **sun reclaim** praying to him 820; *pron.* his 750*n etc.*; **les soens** his people, companions 283

sunt *see* **estre**[1]

super 750, *v.n.* have supper

superbe, *s.* overweening pride 523, 529

sur, *prep.* on 282, 466, 552 *etc.*; over, above 166, 256, 492 *etc.*; up to 833; more than 471*n*, 702*n*, 1675, 1819; (*temporal*) on 134; in addition to 326; *see also* **peis**[2]; *cf.* **surs**[1]

surdre; *ind.pr.3* **surt** 899; *pp.m. nom.sg.* **surs** 1664, *f.pl.* **surses** 1276; *v.n.* arise, happen 899, 1276; open out 1664

surplantez, *pp.adj.m.nom.sg.* set far above 1701

surrist, *pret.3 of* **surrire**, *v.n.* smile 1049

surs[1], *adv.* on it 1384

surs[2] 1664, **surses** 1276 *see* **surdre**

sururer 1604, *v.a.* outstay, fail to take advantage of

survint, *pret.3 of* **survenir**, *v.n.* come into view 1514

sus, *adv.* up 204, 207, 317 *etc.*; on to dry land 386, 968 985; **en s.** upwards 1069; **curre s.** attack, descend on 809; **traire s.** hoist (*sail*) 1808; *see also* **sailir**

suspeis, *s.pl.* judgement 993

sustenir; *ind.impf.3* **susteneit** 1084; *pp.m.obl.pl.* **sustenuz** 737; *v.a.* support 1084; sustain, provide for 737

sustentez, *pp.m.nom.sg. of* **sustenter**, *v.a.* uphold 202

suth *see* **suz**

sutil, *adv.* finely 1073

süurance, *s.* assurance 121

süurs *see* **soür**

suveners, *adj.m.nom.sg.* mindful 1564

suvent, *adv.* often, repeatedly 48, 623, 1164, 1566, 1821

suvereins 562, **suverains** 1676, *adj.m.nom.sg.* supreme: **li s. reis** God

suz 35, 167, **suth** 672 *prep.* under; *cf.* **trone**

t' *see* **tu**

ta *see* **tun**

taceledes, *pp.adj.f.pl. of* **taceler** (= **tacheler**), *v.a.* spot 492

taisir; *ind.pr.3* **taist** 376, 667, 6 **taisent** 698; *pret.3* **tout** 1262; *v.pron.* be silent

talent, *s.*: **li prist t. de** he conceived a desire, had a mind to 47; **metre en t.** fill with the desire, urge (to) 311

tamez, *imper.5 of* **tameir**, *v.pron.* be afraid 457

tant 25 *etc.*; *m.obl.pl.* **tanz** 574, 957, 1440; *f.sg.* **tante** 4, 1044; *f.pl.* **tantes** 958, 1400; *adj.* so great, so much, so many 4, 574, 957 *etc.*; *adv.* so (much) 97, 418, 500 *etc.*; *pron.* so much 25, 807, 993 *etc.*; this much 536; **de t.** by so much 1176; times as much 1791; **t. cum** as much, many as 179, 245, 303 *etc.*; as long as 237, 731, 1829; **t. . . . cum** as . . . as 509, 1356, 1377; **t. quant** as far as 161; **tant . . . que** so far that, until (= and finally) 669; *see also* **itant**; *cf.* **altretant, cum**

tapinage, *s.* hiding, seclusion 723

targer; *v.n. and pron.* delay 135, 619, 845 *etc.*

tart[1], *adv.*: **a t.** long afterwards 635, 653, 981; **a t. li est** he longs (to) 1139; **mei est t.** I long (to) 1393; **sembler, estre t. (a)** find the time long (until), be impatient (to) 1076*n*, 1480

tart², *sbj.pr.3 of* **tarder**, *v.pron*. be slow 384

te, tei *see* **tu**

teinz, *pp.m.nom.sg. of* **teindre**, *v.a.* discolour, blacken 1372

teingent *see* **tenir**

tel 792 *etc.*, **itel** 16, 91, 560 *etc.*, *m.nom.sg.* **tels** 1701; *obl.pl.* **tels** 938, 1046, 1425, 1426, 1438; *adj.* such 16, 91, 560 *etc.*; *pron.* some- (one) 792, 1637; **t.** ... **t.** one ... another, some ... others 812; **t. cum** like, as if 938

tempestes, *s.pl.* storms 970

temptez, *pp.m.nom.sg. of* **tempter**, *v.a.* tempt 201

tenablement, *adv.* fervently, constantly 59

tenailes, *s.pl.* tongs 1145

tendre 233, 610, 1111; *ind.pr.3* **tent** 857, 1008, 1017 *etc.*, 6 **tendent** 209, 967, 1635, 1703; *ind.impf.3* **tendeit** 315; *pp.* **tendud** 826; *v.a.* stretch out 190, 1008, 1017; offer 315; spread (*sail*) 209; pitch (*tent*) 826, 857, 967; direct (*course*) 610, 1635; *v.n.* extend, stretch 255, 1071; distend 1423; head (for), go, set one's course 233, 1111, 1703

tendrunt *see* **tenir**

tenebres, *s.pl.* darkness 323, 1418

tenebrus, *adj.* dark 1122, 1392

tenerge, *s.* darkness 1647

tenir 1522; *ind.pr.6* **tenent** 806; *ind.impf.3* **teneit** 314, 1145, 1226 *etc.*; *fut.6* **tendrunt** 1432; *pret.3* **tint** 1062, 1443, 1513, 6 **tindrent** 34, 816; *sbj.pr.6* **teingent** 1610; *imper.5* **tenez** 1502; *v.a.* possess 314; keep (*faith*) 806; hold 1145, 1432; keep to, continue on (*one's way*) 1062, 1502, 1513; *v.n.*: **faire t.** make fast 1522; *v.pron.* observe, follow 34; consider oneself 816; hold on 1226, 1227, 1443

tens, *sm.* time 595, 785, 859 *etc.*; weather 972, 1554; *cf.* **lunc**

tensor, *s.* treasure 1754; *cf.* **tresor**

tent *see* **tendre**

teons *see* **tun**

terce *see* **terz**

termes, *s.pl.* day, date 891; *see* **metre**

terre, *sf.* land 83, 161, 247 *etc.*; ground 495, 1723; sea-bed 1043; **lei de t.** secular law 3

terz 392, 590, 1498, **tierz** 201; *f.sg.* **terce** 982; *adj.* third 201 *etc* (*cf.* 831, 1087)

testes, *s.pl.* heads 934

tierz *see* **terz**

tindrent, tint *see* **tenir**

tistes, *s.pl.* (ornamental) gospel-books 675

tolir; *ind.pr.3* **tolt** 498, 6 **tolent** 1130; *sbj.pr.3* **tolget** 1758; *imper.4* **toluns** 1092; *pp.* **tolud** 821; *v.a.* remove, blot out 498, 1130, 1758; *v.n. and pron.* leave, go away 821, 1092

ton *see* **tun**

topaze *see* **tupazes**

tors, *s.pl.* bulls 912

tost, *adv.* quickly, soon 318, 356, 428 *etc.*

tot *see* **tut**

tout 1262 *see* **taisir**

trahi *see* **traïr**

traïr; *ind.impf.1* **traïseie** 1266; *pret.1* **trahi** 1282; *v.a.* betray

traire 398, 614, 1201; *ind.pr.3* **trait** 1150, 6 **traient** 488, 855, 904, 968; *sbj.pr.6* **traient** 976; *pret.3* **traist** 929, 932, 6 **trestrent** 380; pp. **trait** 1808, *f.* **traite** 420; *v.a.* suffer, endure 380, 614, 904 *etc.*; pull, drag 398, 488, 855 *etc.*; milk 420; *v.n. and pron.* move 929, 932; *see also* **sus**

traitez, *pp.m.nom.sg. of* **traiter**, *v.a.* treat 1289

tramis, *pp. of* **trametre**, *v.a.* send 396

travaile, *s.* difficulty, hardship 1678

travailez, *pp.subst.obl.pl.* tired travellers 827

travalz 250, 587, **travailz** 1173, *s.pl.* hardships, diffculties

tref¹, *sm.* tent 826, 857, 967, 1077

tref², *s*. beam 1084
treis 134, 260, 327 *etc*., tres 35, 78, 188 *etc*., *num.adj*. three (*cf*. 812, 897, 994)
trenchant *m.nom.pl*. 940; *f.pl*. trenchantes 1010; *pres.p.adj*. sharp 940, 1010; *sm*. cutting edge 1714
trenchéd, *pp. of* trencher, *v.a*. hew, cut 262
trent' 1563, 1576, 1581, 1590, trente 1295, *num.adj*. thirty
tres¹, *adv*. very 143
tres² *num. see* treis
trescurud, *pp. of* trescurre, *v.a*. sail across 438
tresor 316; *obl.pl*. tresors 674; *sm*. treasure; *cf*. tensor
trestrent *see* traire
trestuit *see* trestut
tresturn, *s*. whirling, turning motion 1354; faire t. cease 138
trestut 44, 1305, 1313 *etc*., trestout 893; *m.nom.pl*. trestuit 154, 309, 691; *m.obl.pl*. trestuz 46, 341, 348 *etc*.; *adv*. completely, entirely 893, 1557, 1706; *adj*. all 44, 478, 1313 *etc*.; *pron*. (each and) everyone 46, 154, 309 *etc*.; *cf*. tut
tristur, *s*. dejection, sadness 1175
trone, *sm*. firmament 1241: suth le t. in all the world 672
trop, *adv*. too much 296, 696, 804, 811
trov- *see* truver
truble 644, 1103, 1481; *m.nom.sg*. trubles 754; *adj*. muddy 644, 754; covered in cloud, indistinct 1103; hoarse 1481
truver; *ind.pr.3* trovet 956, *4* truvum 402, trovum 745, *6* truvent 251 261, 630 *etc*., trovent 294, 643, 797 *etc*.; *fut.1* truverai 433, 584, *3* truverat 246, 412, truvrat 1766; *pret.1* truvai 1550, *3* truvat 1823, 1826, trovat 725, *6* truverent 287, 1219; *pp*. trovét 650, 1512; *v.a*. find, discover 251, 261, 294 *etc*.; provide 246, 412, 725 *etc*.

tu 423, 513, 515 *etc*.; *obl*. te 1258, 1319, 1599, t' 192, 1797; *str.obl*. tei 6, 7, 193 *etc*.; *pron*. you (= thou, thee); *see also* tul; *cf*. vus
tüer 1291, *v.a. and refl*. kill 1291, 1298
tuisun, *sf*. fleece 388
tuit *see* tut
tul 14 = tu + le; *cf*. il
tumulte, *s*. commotion, uproar 946
tun 775, ton 191; *f.sg*. ta 424, 426, 774 *etc*.; *str.m.nom.sg*. teons 12; *adj. and pron*. your (= thine)
tuneirs, *sm.nom.sg*. thunderclap 1126
tunes, *sf.pl*. barrels 998
tupazes 685, topaze 1684, *s*. topaz
tur, *sf*. tower 1672
turment 206 *etc*.; *obl.pl*. turmenz 1256; *sm*. storm 206, 624, 916, 1235; torment, punishment 1140, 1350, 1380 *etc*.
turmente 901 *etc*.; *pl*. turmentes 1320, 1466; *sf*. storm 901, 985; torment, suffering 1320, 1395, 1466
turn, *sm*. return journey 874; turn 1088
turner; *v.n. and pron*. be deflected 159; set off, depart 328, 427, 832 *etc*.
turnïer; *ind.pr.1* turni 1356, *3* turnïet 1711; *v.n*. turn, whirl round
tut 141 *etc*., tot 1358, 1360; *m.nom.sg*. tuz 220, 272, 341 *etc*.; *m.nom.pl*. tuit 187, 221, 236 *etc*.; *m.obl.pl*. tuz 108, 149 *etc*.; *f.sg*. tute 455, 499, 747 *etc*.; *f.pl*. tutes 213, 389, 998, 1492, 1675; *adj*. all 141, 149, 175 *etc*.; very 108*n*; any 250; tot dis 1358, tuz dis 591, 1554, 1567 *etc*. always, continually; *pron*. all, everything 321, 324, 412 *etc*.; *adv*. quite, completely 170, 235, 293, 620*n etc*.; *cf*. od, par, parmi, trestut

u¹ 50 *etc*., o 1795, *pron*. where, in

which 50, 56, 86 *etc.*; *adv.* from where 321; where 776, 1157, 1322, 1832

u²,*conj.* or 1040: **u . . . u** either . . . or 1504

ubli, *s.* forgetfulness, negligence 818

ublïer 820, *v.a.* forget 820; *v.pron.* be remiss, fail 305*n*, 844

udurs *see* **odur**

uilz 1138, 1198, **oilz** 407, *s.pl.* eyes

uindre 177*n*, *v.a.* caulk

uit, *num.adj.* eight 605, 615

uitante, *num.adj.* eighty 719, 736

uitaves, *s.pl.* octaves (*week inclusive of festival day*) 586, 778, 862

uitime, *num.adj.* eighth 767

ultre, *prep.* beyond, across 1361

ulurs, *s.pl.* stenches 1425

um 960, 1273 *see* **homme**

umbraiet, *ind.pr.3 of* **umbraier**, *v.n.* cast shade 498

umeit, *s.* boggy ground? 801*n*

un 74 *etc.*; *nom.sg.* **uns** 405, 636, 641 *etc.*; *f.* **une** 47, 263, 277 *etc.*, **un'** 1457; *adj.* one 47, 235, 263 *etc.*; *def.art.* a(n) 74, 93, 166 *etc.*; *pron.* one 310, 353, 399 *etc.*: **uns e uns** one by one 641; **e l'un e l'el** one thing and another (= everything) 1825

unc 159, 224, 418 *etc.*, **unches** 500, 561, 1250, **unckes** 1568, *adv.*: **u. . . . ne** never; *see also* **mais²**

unce, *s.* ounce 1066

unches, unckes *see* **unc**

uncore, *adv.* still, yet 547, 726, 1055, 1098

unde, *s.* wave, water 178, 915, 983 *etc.*

ungle, *s.* claw 1008, 1012

uns *see* **un**

unt¹, *adv.*: **par u.** through which 168

unt² *v. see* **aveir**

urat *see* **urer**

ure 308, 712, 1768, **hure** 844, 1244; *pl.* **hures** 755; *s.* hour, (appointed) time 308, 755, 844*n etc.*; canonical hour 712

uré *see* **oré**

ureisuns, *s.pl.* prayers 138

urer; *pret.3* **urat** 925; *pp.* **urét** 926; *v.a. and n.* pray (for)

usent, *ind.pr.6 of* **user**, *v.n.* wear out 598

ustilz, *s.pl.* gear, implements 179

uverte, *pp.f. of* **uvrir**, *v.a.* open 1727

uvrer, *adj.*: **jurn u.** working day 747

uvrét, *pp. of* **uvrer**, *v.a.* work, embroider 1073

va *see* **aler¹**

vain, *adj.* empty 1568*n*; **nun en v.** with ultimate success 90

vaisele, *sf.* plate, dining-service, vessels 291

vait *see* **aler¹**

val, *sm.* valley 1122, 1123, 1339 *etc.*

valeir; *ind.pr.3* **valt** 1455; *fut.3* **valdrat** 2; *pret.3* **valut** 1830; *v.n.* prevail 2; be of value, help 1455, 1830

valur, *s.* worth 888

vas *see* **aler¹**

vassalment, *adv.* nobly, courageously 114

veablement, *adv.* clearly, openly 60

veables, *adj.nom.sg.* visible 341

veanz *see* **vedeir**

vedeir 664, 1712, 1769, **vetheir** 55, 61, 65, 218; *ind.pr.2* **veis** 423, 1789, **veiz** 1301, 1312, 1372, *3* **veit** 143, 871, 955 *etc.*, *4* **veduns** 744, **veüm** 1043, 1045, *5* **vëez** 1368, *6* **veient** 247, 273, 375; *ind.impf.3* **vetheit** 313, 324, **vedeit** 814; *fut.5* **verrez** 340, 363, 428, 475, *6* **verrunt** 1102; *pret.1* **vi** 418, 1283, 1285 *etc.*, *3* **vit** 83, 102, 108 *etc.*, *5* **veïstes** 751, *6* **virent** 628, 836, 1132 *etc.*; *sbj.pres.5* **veiez** 360, 361; *imper.5* **vedez** 334, **veiez** 987; *pres.p.* **veanz** 348, **veiant** 375, 1022; *pp.* **voüt** 371, 374, **voüd** 1177, **veüd** 559, 1715, 1792; *v.a.* see; *subst.inf.* sight 1712; *pres.p.ger.* before the eyes, in the sight of 348, 1022; *cf.* **veüe**

vedue 493 *see* **veüe**

vilain, *sm.nom.pl.* common people 163

vilement, *adv.* basely, shamefully 1289

vinc, vindrent, vint *see* **venir**

vint, *num.adj.* twenty 717

virent *see* **vedeir**

virun, *adv. and prep.* around 631, 801

vis¹, *sm.* face 1225, 1453

vis², *s.* opinion: **m'est (li est) vis** it seems to me (him) 1395, 1397, 1587

vit *see* **vedeir**

vitaile, *s.* food, provisions 237

vitte, *sf.* (saintly) life 76

vivere 956; *ind.pr.4* **vivum** 761; *pret.3* **vesquit** 731; *pp.* **vescut** 408, 1589; *v.n.* live; *subst.inf.* food, sustenance 956

voices *see* **voiz**

voi(s) *see* **aler¹**

voil(e) *see* **voleir**

voiz 1037, 1263, 1481; *pl.* **voiz** 189, **voices** 557; *sf.* voice

vol 869, 1018; *nom.sg.* **vols** 509; *sm.* flight; *see also* **voler**

voleir; *ind.pr.1* **voil** 118, *3* **volt** 766; *ind.impf.3* **voleit** 148, 474, *6* **voleient** 696; *fut.3* **voldrat** 72, 80, 144, 871, 1770; *cond.3* **voldreit** 61; *sbj.pr.3* **voile** 17; *pret.3* **volt** 155, 299, 325 *etc.*, *6* **voldrent** 293, 604, 1296; **voldret** 55n; *v.a. and n.* wish, desire, want

voler; *ind.pr.1* **vol** 1361, *3* **volet** 936, *6* **volent** 1124, 1129; *v.n.* fly

volt *see* **voleir**

volunters, *adv.* gladly, willingly 772, 961, 1536

voluntét, *sf.* will 1764

voluntif, *adj.* eager, desirous 87

vomir 1421, *v.n.* vomit

vos *see* **vus**

vostre 763, 874, 878, 1502; *obl.pl.* **voz** 860, 993, 1052; *adj.* your

voüd, voüt *see* **vedeir**

voz *see* **vostre**

vunt *see* **aler**

vus 199, 201, 225 *etc.*, **vos** 117, 118, 119 *etc.*, *pron.* you, your; *cf.* **ast**

werec, *sm.* wrack, sea-weed 1571

Index of proper names

All names occurring within the text are listed together with their variants. Line references are exhaustive. The letter *n* refers to the Notes to the text.